When the Air Comes Out of the Ball

JR INMAN

SECOND EDITION 2023

Copyright © 2023 Jr Inman.

All rights reserved. No part of this book may be reproduced, stored, or transmitted by any means—whether auditory, graphic, mechanical, or electronic—without written permission of both publisher and author, except in the case of brief excerpts used in critical articles and reviews. Unauthorized reproduction of any part of this work is illegal and is punishable by law.

ISBN: 979-8-88640-722-8 (sc)
ISBN: 979-8-88640-723-5 (hc)
ISBN: 979-8-88640-724-2 (e)

Because of the dynamic nature of the Internet, any web addresses or links contained in this book may have changed since publication and may no longer be valid. The views expressed in this work are solely those of the author and do not necessarily reflect the views of the publisher, and the publisher hereby disclaims any responsibility for them.

One Galleria Blvd., Suite 1900, Metairie, LA 70001
1-888-421-2397

CONTENTS

Acknowledgments vii

Introduction ix

Chapter 1   The Young Athlete 1

Chapter 2   The College Student Athlete 13

Chapter 3   Injuries to the Body and Mind 26

Chapter 4   Climbing Over the Hill 38

Chapter 5   AA Counseling (Athletics and Academics) 45

Chapter 6   Goals Grant Greatness 56

Chapter 7   Giving Back 64

Chapter 8   Inmanology 101 77

Chapter 9   The Perks of Being a Ballplayer 84

Chapter 10   From Black Kicks to Hard Bottoms 91

Chapter 11   JR's Final Thoughts 102

References 105

TABLE OF FIGURES

Figure 1: Tyrell Biggs (Don Bosco Preparatory High School's Alltime Leading Scorer and Childhood Friend of Jr Inman)..8

Figure 2: JR Inman, Westchester Knicks, NBA G League...............9

Figure 3: Paul Robeson (Rutgers University) 14

Figure 4: JR Inman in Rutgers vs. Kansas State, 2006...................14

Figure 5: JR Inman defends Tyler Hansbrough in Rutgers vs. North Carolina (December 2008). "This was my senior year when we played UNC at the Dean Smith Center. I was mic'd up on campus two days leading up to the game. In a quote heard around the basketball world of collegiate hoops, I coined the punchline "Tyler Hansbrough my hands are thorough."..................18

Figure 6: SMART Goals Chart...21

Figure 7: The Kuhn Cycle 23

Figure 8: Picture of the skeletal bone structure of a leg. I was forced to play with a severely bruised fibula, which in turn broke as a result of constant overuse and pressure 30

Figure 9: Gerald H. Inman Jr. on Graduation Day, Rutgers University Class of 2009....................................50

Figure 10: 2002 Saint Joseph Regional High School Men's
Basketball Team (Jason, Devin, and JR Inman)............... 59

Figure 10.1: JR Inman, Bergen County Jamboree, Winter 2002...... 59

Figure 10.2: JR Inman, SJR Alumni Basketball, Winter 2023 59

Figure 11: JR Inman and Hamaday N'Diaye against Syracuse
University (2007 Rutgers Men's Basketball Season)......... 61

Figure 11.1: Hamaday N'Diaye, Rokee, Sacramento Kings,
NBA Drive, 2010 61

Figure 12: JR Inman, League Commissioner,
JCC Premiere Basketball League, Spring 2023 63

Figure 13: JR "throwing it down" in Kyoto, Japan vs.
Okinawa (Winter 2009) 63

Figure 14: Inmanology 101 at Rocktown Basketball Academy
"Each one, teach one, grab one, reach one"
(Regional Sainte-Rose).. 65

Figure 15: JR Inman, Mark Jenkins, and Kenny Smith
(Omega Psi Phi Fraternity, Inc. TZ FALL '08)................. 68

Figure 16: JR inside the Church of Mensa Christi 85

ACKNOWLEDGMENTS

Giving honor to God who is the head of my life. To my loving parents: the late Gerald Inman Sr. and Deborah Inman, as well as my sister, Jasmine Inman. Honoring and remembering my late grandmother Annie Jewel Williams; my former Pastor Dr. Reverend Willie L. Hairston; and the high school alumni of Saint Joseph Regional High School (Montvale, NJ). Also to my good friends on the Banks of the Old Raritan at Rutgers University. As a proud alumnus of these great schools, I am forever indebted to the resources you have granted as well as the empowerment that you've instilled in me.

I'd also respectfully acknowledge my childhood coaches: Kevin Buno (Rockland Ravens), Michael Doherty, Reginald Sainte-Rose, and Thomas Reedy, as well as all of Saint Joseph Regional HS affiliates. I'd also like to recognize Coaches Keith and Kelvin Smith (Gauchos, NYC), Jimmy Salmon (NJ Legacy), and Kent Kulluko (IYB Basketball). Coaches Gary Waters and Larry Desimpelare (Rutgers University), Kevin Whitted, Craig Hodges, Allan Houston (Westchester Knicks), and David Benoit (Utah Jazz, Kyoto Hannaryz).

Each of these men has taught me something not only about basketball but also about the fundamentals of life, legacy, faith, and friendship.

To the brotherhood of Omega Psi Phi Fraternity Inc., I'd like to also acknowledge and salute my dean, the Honorable Sloan Toussaint Baptist as well as my line brothers, Bro. Kenny Smith and Bro. Mark Jenkins. I salute you as well as the entire Tau Zeta and Xi Lambda

Lambda Chapters! Thank you for pumping pillars of excellence in my bloodstream.

To my family at Kaplen JCC and Palisades: Tenafly, NJ. I give honors to Hagit Tal, Keri Thoren, and Raychel Reilly who made it possible for me to fertilize my soil on stable ground and now we are all living to see this glorious dream manifest. Thank you for being a foundation of BallerZ Elite Basketball which is one of my greatest creations!

To the Inman, Hunter, Carmichael, Mcleod, Augustin, Ramos, and Biggs families. Thank you for being an extension of my family tree. You all have also taught me valuable lessons about life, love, leadership and so much more. And last and undoubtedly not least, I sincerely dedicate, honor, and recognize my precious first born, Melodia Grace Inman. May God continue to pour down and rain mercy upon you for all the days you shall live! You are the source of my contentment and hope for all I do. Daddy will always love you, never leave you, and continue to provide the best for you that I possibly can. To all of my readers, who saw the title and cover page and had enough curiosity to show interest in my life story . . . thank you!

INTRODUCTION

We all come from different cultures and backgrounds. Within these different cultures are customs that people follow. My upbringing as a middle-class student athlete is one that placed a high regard of importance on both academics as well as athletics. In all of my years hooping, it was typical for me to come across players who were nearsighted—never thinking past the days when their playing days would come to an end. It is in these moments when you should ask yourself, "What will I do with my life *when the air comes out of the ball?*"

When the Air Comes Out of the Ball is a simple metaphor. If I was a tennis player, I could have easily named it *When the Strings Come Out of the Racket*. For all dancers reading this story, what will you do *When the Tap Comes Out of the Shoe?* For every tennis player will swing their last racquet, and every dancer will strut their final dance.

The game of basketball has been oh so good to me as it has taught me many valuable lessons! Over time I've learned to grasp every lesson learned the same way I clench a basketball. My palms grasp every dribble I take on the court whether moving forward, or backward. Every dribbling moment should be used to guide your intuition to move forward toward achieving your personal goals.

Life, my friend, won't always be a crystal stair. In times when confusion may result in missed opportunities, setbacks, and personal struggles, one must always remember to stay focused and stick to the plan. Set your own precedent and always hold yourself accountable first before anyone else. Work hard to provide for your family. For there comes a time when every athlete must understand that there is more to life, than sprints, drills, warm-ups, and game strategy.

This treasuring document provides insight into the mindset an athlete must have in order to succeed and cross over into the next stage of life. Development all in itself is inevitable, for the days we stop growing and enhancing as individuals are the days when our souls begin to perish. After all, basketball is just a game, right? Wrong! Basketball is a vehicle that can jumpstart your life while allowing you to venture along highways, byways, twists, and turns while enduring and persevering through the whips and scorns of time.

When you are young and your parents put a ball into your hand for the first time, at first it just appears to be a round orange object with black lines running through it. Then you bounce it once or twice and before you know it you're playing basketball. That first feeling you felt as if you'd say, "Hey, this thing is kinda cool." What you didn't realize at that moment is that you just started playing a game that will never stop being played until the end of time.

For young hoopers, it's a joyful experience; to have a hobby that you may practice every once in a while and at the same time have fun playing with friends around your neighborhood or in school. It is only as you grow older that you begin to see all the benefits of playing this precious game that it may possibly offer.

For all parents reading this part of my story, please pause and consider the various talents your child(ren) may have. Make a pledge to yourself to fully invest the time, care, and consideration it takes to support your children's wildest dreams. Afterward, please devote your time on a daily basis to instill proper ethics and principles into your children in hopes this might ensure that they can someday grow to become diplomatically functioning individuals in society. I am asking this of you because that is what my parents always provided for me.

I was privileged to have a middle/upper-class upbringing. I was raised by both parents in a beautiful home in a suburb twenty minutes outside of New York City (Rockland County, NY). My supportive mother, Deborah Inman, is described as a nurturing, caring person, whose love can be felt by all those who come into contact with her. She instilled moral values in me that I'll always carry with me throughout the days of my life. My mother has taught me how to lead by example with honesty, integrity, dignity, and pride. It is because of her that I possess the compassion to help others and share deep moments of empathy.

My endearing late father, Gerald Inman Sr., was considered by many a "Manly Man." He was stern, upright, and circumspect in stature. My father strategically played defensive end at 6'5, 285 lbs. for the San Francisco 49ers. After foregoing a mandated serious surgery which shortened his promising football career, my dad was forced to retire. However, my father did not and would not allow a devastating football injury to become catastrophic and end his success in life. *When the air came out of his ball*, my father began pursuing and establishing his successful career in business where he began working for Merry Lynch in the 1980s. In combination, my dad was greatly influenced by his professional football career and his unforgettable legacy of over thirty-five years on Wall Street. This taught him a great deal. My father inspired me at a young age to become strong and never play around, dream, and/or drift. I owe all of my life to him and my mother for the valuable lessons they both have taught me from day one. This is why I am professing my story to you.

CHAPTER 1

The Young Athlete

In the early stages of a child's development, parents begin to think of various activities their child can become involved in that would help mold a sense of belonging and purpose. When I was younger, I liked to experience many things. These encounters enabled me to constructively participate in a variety of events. This brought out the potential of a multitude of my innate skills. When I was a youngster, my parents mandated that my sister and I attend and participate in weekly church services. As a positive result, the Holy Spirit molded my young fast-paced mind which led me to pursue many constructive activities and worthy events and affairs. At times I would meditate and separate my strengths from my weaknesses. This enabled me to reflect from an insightful lens that exposed God's true intentions He had for my life to me at a very young age.

I started participating in sports when I was eight years old. Little did I know that this game would affect and direct my life for as long as I shall live. During my first year, I played for Team Valley Cottage in the Haverstraw Police Athletic League. My Father was my first coach. Coach Gerald Inman Sr. was a very demanding coach who stressed hard work and "smash mouth" defense. In that first year playing, I had an undeveloped skill set but showed glaring flashes of strong potential. Spearheading my passion for the game, my father taught me to approach everything I do with a serious mindset. When you relate this concept to basketball, you learn how to approach every game you play, as if it is your last. It was very soon after the start of my first season that basketball became a major priority in my life.

I can still remember the first blooper in my career. It was then I realized just how serious the game of basketball can be. It was a regular season game against our archrivals from Haverstraw, New York. My teammates and I represented Valley Cottage, New York. The fellows on my team knew some of the kids from the opposing team and both teams had a reputation of being at the top of the ranks in the entire league. This game sparked the attention of many fans. They came out to cheer and support both sides. I remembered being a tad bit nervous because a girl whose name was "K" was sitting courtside during this game with her sister Mel and two other girls.

In the third quarter, I had a fast break routine layup. Distracted by the cheers from my schoolyard girl friends, I took my eyes off the rim and shot a layup that barely grazed the front of the rim. To hide my most embarrassing and shameful moment, I did pretty much what any other average kid would do and that was to play it off and laugh. As I ran back down the court with a smirk on my face, I looked over to my father who was not pleased by my lackadaisical error. He instantly subbed me out of the game and explained to me why he made the lineup change. Although I didn't understand why my father was so aggravated, I respectfully listened to his advice and took heed of his decision.

This taught me that everything you do in life should be done with great passion. With this passion comes responsibility to focus and eagerness to strive for perfection. There may be many times in your life when you feel embarrassed or as if you've failed. Learn from your shortcomings but do not let them weigh you down. Develop improvisions that will convert your weaknesses into your strengths. This is when persevering becomes vitally important.

During my senior year in college, I was sworn into the Omega Psi Phi Fraternity, Inc., LLC. I inherited the values and beliefs of men who lived by the code of perseverance. My line brothers and I were taught that "effort only releases its true reward after one refuses to quit" (Showbiz Dog Fall 06, Duce Tail). This concept of perseverance was something I encompassed in my younger years, but I didn't begin to appreciate its true meaning until my later years.

In seventh grade, I entered into the next phase of my athletic career. I was introduced to the game of football. As the son of a retired NFL defensive lineman, football was always a part of my family's culture. Once again my father suffered from a career-ending shoulder injury in his first season playing for the San Francisco 49ers. His injury made both of my parents extremely paranoid about my participation in such a vigorous contact sport. Nevertheless, they allowed me to make my own decision on whether or not I would try out for the team. This was not the easiest thing for me because I attended a new school and was surrounded by kids that I didn't really know. What made things even more difficult was that I had never played organized football before. I didn't even know how to put on a jockstrap.

At my first practice, I was utilized in a number of positions. My physique and natural motor skills enabled me to be useful on both sides of the football team. Within the first week of practice, I displayed leadership skills and a height advantage over my opponents. These intangibles were pivotal in our team's success as I earned the position of starting quarterback on the seventh grade team. Being a rookie quarterback on a team that had experienced players in all other positions wasn't the easiest thing to do.

I always had faith that God would see me through all of my struggling obstacles. It is my belief that he put me in a position to lead others who were older and more experienced than I was to test my heart and willpower. As a seventh grader, my natural skills were so evident that the coach promoted me to the backup quarterback position on the eighth grade team.

Pomona Middle School always had a reputation for having a fierce competitive football program. To be promoted to the eighth grade team as a rookie seventh grader was an honor. There were many players on the seventh grade team who envied the opportunity I had, but I did not let that distract me.

It was then I learned another valuable lesson. "Many are called, but few are chosen" (Matt. 22:14). Sometimes God chooses us at times in our lives when we feel as if we are not ready to carry out his duty. It is our duty as believers, to fulfill the opportunities we are given in life to the best of our abilities.

After the football season, I would learn another valuable lesson during the Thanksgiving holiday. Anyone who grew up playing high school basketball knows that this is when you lace up the kicks, put on the old tank top, and bring out the leather ball in preparation for a long season on the hardwood.

Basketball season was coming, and I was very excited to take the skills I learned from my father and transfer them from a recreational league into a grammar school style of play. My excitement for the upcoming season vanished after I received my first report card for the fall 2000 marking period. After failing three classes, I was declared academically ineligible to participate in the winter 2000–2001 basketball season.

Facing embarrassment for the second time in my athletic career, I began to understand that the humiliation I felt from my lack of success on the court and my failure to comply with school academic policy, were equally dissatisfying. I had to clean up my act! I realized that in academic institutions, scholastics and athletics go hand in hand. I graduated from an institution of knowledge that holds accountable those who don't perform well in the classroom. If any student athlete reaches the status of academically ineligible, then they won't be granted the opportunity to compete on any athletic team.

During the entire winter 2000 season, I began to change my outlook on school. I started studying every night, handing in my homework assignments on time, and sitting in the front in all of my classes. At the end of the next marking period, my grades were elevated which gave me the opportunity to try out for spring sports.

When the Air Comes Out of the Ball

In the springtime, sports fans tend to take a break from the hardwood and turn their attention toward the green grass and dirt mound fields of baseball. Growing up, I always took pride in being a multifaceted athlete. The love I had for athletic competition led me to try out for the Pomona Middle School baseball team. Having little experience in the game of baseball, I had yet another obstacle to overcome.

The baseball coach felt that I would be most beneficial to the team as a pitcher. I was always taller than my peers. My height advantage gave me leverage over my opponents in all sports. My childhood friends would compare my presence on the mound to the Hall of Fame pitcher Randy Johnson. Although I didn't have a ninety-mile-per-hour fastball, I was a tall, slinky, heavy-handed pitcher who would throw pitches and make the catcher's glove pop like popcorn. I felt that I resembled Randy Johnson's physical traits minus the difference in skin complexion. I firmly believed that playing the most significant roles in two different sports (football quarterback and baseball pitcher) was ironic. I felt that this was an early sign that I was blessed with gifts of versatility and transformative leadership.

One of the most valuable lessons I learned in baseball is that every position in every sport requires technique and focus. This enables one to perform at a high level of play during game competitions. While glamorous sports rhetoric can sometimes be more appealing, there are life lessons that come with excruciating pain.

It was a breezy afternoon, which is pretty typical for a spring midday baseball practice. I was playing third base during a routine infield defensive drill. The coach would hit the balls at the first baseman, whose job was to throw it to me on a direct line as hard as he could. I would catch the ball before the base runner reached third base. But that day, I used the wrong technique while trying to catch the baseball. When the first baseman threw the ball toward me, it tipped off the end of my glove and struck me directly in the face, knocking out my right front tooth and pushing two other teeth into my gums.

As I was rushed to the dentist, I thought, ***How could this happen to me?*** As I replayed the scene in my head, I remembered that I had not been focused on catching the ball the right way. That was the reason the ball hit me in the face. Thank God for root canals. I was worried I would be walking around with no front teeth at all. Even so, I still have the permanent memory of what happens in sports when you're not focused on the task at hand.

It was at that point in my young sports career, that I learned three valuable lessons from three different sports. Basketball taught me to take the game very seriously. Football taught me that many are called but only a few are chosen, and baseball taught me that when trying to achieve an individual task, there is a level of focus that is required. One of the most important things all sports have in common is the amount of attention to detail required for excellence. Focus is described as a central point of attraction, attention, or activity one embellishes in. Focus allows us to efficiently function as productive individuals in our society.

Think of all the distractions you experience on a daily basis. There are so many things in our lives that are unnecessary. These things that seemingly have no purpose but to prevent us from getting things done.

When you are focused on your priorities, your brain does not allow these distractions to interrupt your meditation. Thus sports strengthen the mind which gives you the ability to get things done accurately and accordingly.

In high school, I made the decision to narrow my hobbies down to the sport that I had the most passion for: basketball. As a freshman, I played on the freshman and junior varsity team at Saint Joseph Regional High School in Montvale, New Jersey. Parents of the upperclassmen on the varsity team pleaded with my coach, asking him to move me up to the varsity team for the upcoming season.

My parents felt that basketball, like everything else, has a maturation process. Being that I was only fourteen years of age, my father and mother believed that I should play on a team where I could grow and socialize with my peers.

At the time I didn't understand why they didn't want me to play varsity, but as I matured and grew older I began to understand that was a wise decision. This taught me yet another lesson. Many of my friends were also involved with sports at my school and other schools around the tristate area. One of the most heralded freshmen in metro hoops history was a six-foot-six, three-hundred-pound court killer named Tyrell Biggs out of Don Bosco Preparatory High School.

Figure 1: Tyrell Biggs (Don Bosco Preparatory High School's All-time Leading Scorer and Childhood Friend of Jr Inman)

Figure 2: JR Inman, Westchester Knicks, NBA G League.

I would subconsciously compare myself to him because naturally I always wanted to be the best. I felt that if I compared myself to the best then I could be the best. I remember asking my freshman basketball coach Reginald Sainte-Rose what any other kid in my position would ask: "Why can't I play on the varsity team as a freshman?" Coach Sainte-Rose loved my competitive drive. His response was always the same: "JR, you will get everything you need and deserve in your own time." As a young athlete, I could not understand this. My mother once instructed me to reflect on Ecclesiastes 3:1–9. This excerpt helped me understand Sainte-Rose's response:

> [1]"There is a time for everything, and a season for every activity under heaven: [2]a time to be born and a time to die, a time to plant and a time to uproot, [3]a time to kill and a time to heal, a time to tear down and a time to build, [4]a time to weep and a time to laugh, a time to mourn and a time to dance, [5]a time to scatter stones and a time to gather them, a time to embrace and a time to refrain, [6]a time to search and a time to give up, a time to keep and a time to throw away, [7]a time to tear and a time to mend, a time to be silent and a time to speak, [8]a time to love and a time to hate, a time for war and a time for peace. [9]What does the worker gain from his toil?"

God allows all of us to experience our own situations, which are different from everyone else's conditions. As competitive creatures, we sometimes try to compare ourselves to others and live up to their standards. In fact, we despise people who appear to have things that we do not have. As a product of a Christian household, I believe that everything happens for a reason. God works at his own pace. We must have faith in Him that He will deliver unto us, and this is when we reap His blessings.

As I grew older, I continued receiving much instruction from my parents and my coaches. In the spring of my freshman year in high school, I began to train to be a Division 1 athlete. My training began in the Richard Rhoda Center, better known as "The Biddy Gym" in Teaneck, New Jersey. Training under the guidance of Mr. Lincoln Sessoms, I challenged myself to raise the level of my athleticism to an extreme. This period of training not only raised my physical toughness but also elevated my mental toughness as well. Lincoln taught me valuable lessons in life.

Amongst all, he got me to believe and understand that if you want anything in life, you have to work extremely hard for it. I'll never forget his most adamant words of advice, "JR, don't be afraid to be the man. Don't be afraid to be a star."

This is when I began to see the potential he saw in me as an elite basketball player. Devoting my entire spring and summer to hard work and the effective use of it, I entered my junior year of high school with a vengeance. I had the desire to punish my opponents from the start of the game to the finish. Averaging eighteen points, ten rebounds, three blocks, and three steals as a junior, I started to attract scouts, college coaches, and the attention that would place "JR Inman" in the national spotlight.

Coach John Thompson III at Georgetown University was one of the first to recruit me in high school. He told me that I had a really smooth game and great fundamentals. These skills were developed motor skills mastered through repetition and poise. Poise is a vital point in every sport. Players who have poise stand out among their peers because their coaches can count on them to produce under pressure or in adverse situations.

In Coach John Wooden's book, *"The Pyramid of Success,"* he speaks of poise and its relevance to the game of basketball.

> Most people think of poise as calm self-assured dignity, but I call it just being you. When we have poise we're not acting, faking, or pretending. We're not trying to be something we're not, nor are we attempting to live

up to others' expectations. When we are being who we really are, we are more likely to function closer to our own level of competency. (Wooden and Carty 2009, 82)

Sports can sometimes bring out the innermost feelings of intimidation and pressure. Media and the social responsibility athletes have today made it even harder to stay poised during competition. Now more than ever, players are scrutinized and berated because of the effect of public opinion. This is why it is very important to approach sports with an attitude of focus and poise. It is not an easy concept to grasp, but the experiences athletes go through during years and years of antagonism equip them with the poise necessary to be productive.

As the 2004 spring semester of my junior year in high school continued, I received scholarship offers from many top-level schools around the country: Georgia Tech, Maryland, Connecticut, Georgetown, West Virginia, Saint Joseph's, North Carolina State, University of Southern California, and Rutgers. The relationship that men's basketball coach Gary Waters established with my parents, made my decision to attend Rutgers University a no-brainer.

That following summer, I was fortunate to participate in the Adidas All-American Basketball Camp in Suane, Georgia, and the Five-Star Basketball Camp in Pennsylvania. I remember putting on an extraordinary performance. Spectators in the crowd started to ask, "Where's that kid going to school next year?" Many were perplexed by my decision to choose Rutgers over other big-time basketball programs that were recruiting me. Staying close to home was the biggest reason I chose to attend Rutgers University. After being named First Team All-State in New Jersey in my Junior and Senior seasons in high school, I felt practically obligated to raise my talents to the next level of prominence in New Jersey basketball history. My decision to attend Rutgers was one that would have a drastic impact on the rest of my life.

CHAPTER 2

The College Student Athlete

When the fall 2006 school semester started, I was on a college campus for the first time in my life. I was anxious to experience things that every typical college freshman wants to do. Through all of this fun and excitement, I forgot the reason why I was in school. Thank God for a mother who instilled in me the principles and importance of education. She would always tell me that "knowledge is power." I used to laugh whenever she would say that, but the older I got, the more I realized the truth in her message. I entered my first semester at school nervous and not knowing what to expect. It was a struggle for me academically as I developed problems with balancing my school work, basketball, and social life.

I took twelve credits my first semester and practiced six times a week for approximately five months straight. Going through this hectic schedule was very hard as I battled homesickness, physiological sickness, stress, and sports-related injuries.

By the end of my freshman year, things were looking pretty good. I told myself that I wanted to model after the late great Rutgers grad and student athlete Paul Robeson.

Figure 3: Paul Robeson (Rutgers University)

Figure 4: JR Inman in Rutgers vs. Kansas State, 2006

I finished my first year of college with a 2.9 grade point average and received freshman All-American honors. It was at age eighteen that I started to think about my purpose on God's green earth. I would always talk with God, asking Him what He wanted me to do with my life. He would always speak to me through other people, most of whom would tell me that regardless of what I decide to do with my life, if I kept the faith and focused on striving to succeed with an ambitious attitude, then I would become successful.

I began to question what the term *success* meant. Success to me means the attainment of wealth, positions, honors, or other personal achievements. This is a very broad definition that I conceptualized. To help further define the definition of success, I will turn to John Wooden's book *Coach Wooden's Pyramid of Success*. It was here that I found a definition that made the concept of success seem clear to me: "a peace of mind that is the direct result of self-satisfaction in knowing you did your best to become the best that you are capable of becoming" (Wooden and Carty 2009, 17).

Defining success can be very difficult because so many people rely on public opinion to determine whether they are successful or not. When thinking about the true meaning of success, keep in mind that it comes from within. If you are satisfied with your performance and abilities, then you are successful. Besides, the only true judge over man is God himself. On judgment day, he decides whether or not you will successfully ascend to heaven or be burned in the depths of hell.

The amount of pressure put on athletes in today's world by the media and so many other critics is ridiculous. A young athlete who doesn't value his intrapersonal feelings can get distracted by outside sources.

In its simplest form, the most evident man-made representation of success that a college student athlete can achieve is a diploma as you've earned your degree.

Sports are fun and should be enjoyed, but the purpose of attending any university in America is to get that piece of paper that everyone who goes to college strives so hard to earn. To be honest, if your sole purpose is to attend college on an athletic scholarship, then school is not for you. You're probably better off trying out for a semi-professional sports team. Those who play college sports with no intention of graduating are wasting years of their careers and earning potential. They could be getting paid monthly salaries, if the salary is their goal. Throughout my time as a college student athlete, I've seen more athletes get exploited by the system of college sports than you would believe.

How many times have you heard of an athlete's expulsion from school for violating university and team academic and athletic policies? Most academic departments know when kids are in bad academic standings from the beginning. It is sad how some of these kids get pushed through the education system until the school cannot use their athletic abilities any longer. Once their eligibility is up, the school kicks them right out the door and provides limited resources to further support their transition into the real world.

If I had any advice for high school student athletes, I would tell them not to let any system label and control them. In life, sometimes you don't even get a chance to get ahead, but if you're lucky to be dealt a good hand, how you play that hand is completely up to you. Essentially, you must will yourself across that graduation stage. No coach, teacher, parent, or adviser can do it for you. ***It must be up to you and only you!***

In my sophomore year of college, I went through an academic experience that nearly ruined my chances of ever receiving a degree at Rutgers University. My teammates and I were accused in an academic scandal that caused me and two other team members to be suspended indefinitely. Sharing answers to an exam with my teammates wasn't the best thing to do, but because of the time period of the semester and the situation that was at hand, my fellow teammates and I thought it was best if we exchanged ten questions of a final exam for our introduction to sociology class. After the teacher reviewed all of the class exams, he realized that there were three papers that had the same errors for the first ten questions of the exam.

The night before the final take-home exam was due, I had gone over to spend the night with my girlfriend on Bush Campus in the "Suites" at Rutgers University. The next morning, I looked in my bookbag and saw that my exam paper was not there. Not remembering that I had left it in my room under the dresser, I called my teammates and asked them if they had an extra copy of the answers. We exchanged papers and handed in the exam the next day during class.

Luckily my teacher had mercy on us. It was only ten answers out of an eighty-question exam. He was disappointed in us, because he saw the potential in us as students, and was shocked that we exchanged answers. He promised that he would keep this issue in house and not tell higher authorities. Luckily my coach spoke with the professor and told him that we would be suspended one game for violating the team's academic policy. This punishment was minimal compared to the worst-case scenario that could have derived from this transgression. My parents were extremely disappointed about my decision and could not understand how this all came about. I can still remember my parents telling me how they did not raise me to be a sneaky cheater. The shame my parents had as a result of my stupidity caused me to make a pact with myself to never cheat again in my life.

Figure 5: JR Inman defends Tyler Hansbrough in Rutgers vs. North Carolina (December 2008). "This was my senior year when we played UNC at the Dean Smith Center. I was mic'd up on campus two days leading up to the game. In a quote heard around the basketball world of collegiate hoops, I coined the punchline "Tyler Hansbrough my hands are thorough."

After my sophomore year, I earned a few accolades on the court, such as making the Third Team All-Metropolitan Area. I was pleased that my numbers (twelve points and seven rebounds) were among the top leaders for players in my position in the country. My grade point average in my sophomore year was a mediocre 2.5. I made a vow to myself to devote the entire summer toward taking my life to the next level on and off the court.

The summer of my sophomore year was the longest, hardest summer I've ever been through. Determined to take my game and academics to another level, I developed strategies that would allow me to raise the level of my performance. I told myself that I must have two major priorities this summer: basketball and school. Every day I would do something that would directly or indirectly help me better myself in the classroom and on the basketball court. After finishing the first two summer sessions with a 3.4 grade point average and declaring my major in communications in mass media, I packed my bags and headed out to the sweet city of San Francisco. The trip to Cali was yet again another life-changing experience. Training in a new place with different people can make you grow up really fast especially if you are not familiar with the customs, culture, traditions, and values.

During my days in San Fran, a typical day for me would start at six in the morning. I was taught by Frank Matriscino that you must eat healthy so that your body has enough nutrients to perform at a high level for a long period of time. I would usually start off my day with six hard-boiled eggs (no yolks), brown rice, a supplement bar, and bread with naturally flavored jelly. Occasionally, I would eat snacks like grapes, bananas, and nutritional shakes to replenish myself throughout the day. My goal was to maintain muscle mass and eat healthy so that I could vastly improve my overall health and nutrition. Then I would work all day, every day, running the sandy beaches with a weight vest on my back and weights in my hands.

Over the course of that summer, I trained with other NBA players such as Hilton Armstrong of the New Orleans Hornets, Kareem Rush of the Indiana Pacers, and Gabe Pruitt of the Boston Celtics, as well as high school standouts Jordan Hamilton (later drafted to the Denver Nuggets) and Renaldo Sydney. Battling every day with those guys taught me that those who truly want to be successful in life will put in the extra work to reach their aspirations. I looked at the lifestyle of a professional athlete and imagined what it would be like if I lived that life.

Making the NBA was always a goal of mine; however, having a backup plan was even more important. One of my favorite musical performing artists, Styles P, expressed this concept in one of his songs. It's always best "to have a plan A, plan B, even a plan C" (D Block, speakerphone). This code taught me that establishing a strategy for being successful is important, but preparing yourself with alternatives will assure your success. My education was the assurance I needed to implement provisions not only in my basketball career but also in my adult livelihood.

As summer 2007 came to a close, I returned to the East Coast with the determination to have another stellar year in the classroom and on the basketball court. In some ways, I began to see the result of what happens when student athletes fail to meet the academic requirements necessary to stay eligible for competition. It always pierces my soul when I see student athletes drop out of school. Academics and college sports come hand in hand. You can't have one without the other. As athletes, it is important to understand that you just don't attend school to play sports or to waste your time. Going to college gives you a social edge and puts you in a respected social position in society.

There is an inconvenient truth we must all come to terms with at some point in our lives. Indeed friends in this cruel world, life is designed for some people to succeed and others to fail. There cannot be a top without a bottom. This is an inconvenient truth and an unfortunate reality of life in America. I will turn to a legendary social theory called Murphy's Law to help iterate the necessity for having a backup plan in life:

> A supposed law of nature, expressed in various humorous popular sayings, to the effect that anything that can go wrong will go wrong. It is named for Captain Edward A. Murphy, who performed studies on deceleration for the US Air Force in 1949. At this time he noted that if things could be done wrongly, they would be. (Knowles, Murphy's Law)

Murphy believed that when performing tasks, it is human nature for error to occur. When you have a plan of action, it is important to follow it wholeheartedly. Even when taking the proper steps to obtain your goals, the possibility of failure is high and many times inevitable. To prevent yourself from disappointment, set SMART goals, and take the necessary steps toward achieving them.

When the Air Comes Out of the Ball

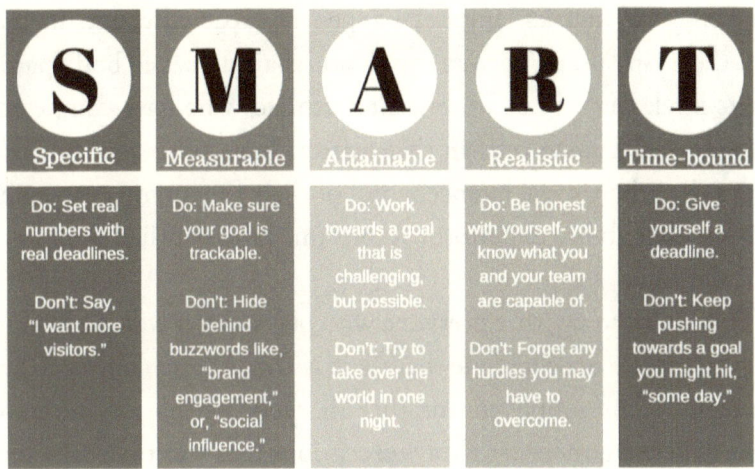

Figure 6: SMART Goals Chart

The SMART goal acronym has been vital in providing a roadmap with how to achieve my goals. When you have an objective in mind, use this thought process to create a strategy. Follow this closely and your success rate will be high.

In basketball specifically, I coach kids all the time and when I ask them what their goal in life is, they respond, "To make it to the NBA." Whenever they respond this way, I always chuckle. I laugh because while it sounds peachy keen, to be selected to play amongst the world's best basketball players, the process to get there is long, grueling, and very time-consuming. Young players have no idea what it takes to make it to the top level and so, just dreaming of your goal but having no plan for achievement is a waste of time.

At the end of the day, all you can do is try. Have faith that your visions will become realities. That is all we can do as imperfect humans. Nothing more, nothing less.

Many athletes have aspirations of playing their sport at the professional level. While this should be every young athlete's goal, it should also be understood that the odds of making it in sports are against you. Statistically, less than 3 percent of all student athletes who compete in college will have an opportunity to play professional sports. One of the leading causes of collegiate athletes ending their careers after college is injuries. Injuries happen unexpectedly, and in many cases, there isn't much doctors can do to repair damaged body parts to an elite level. Maybe not all, but most athletes who have competed in college sports at some time in their careers have either had surgery or injuries that change the biomechanics of their functioning movement, affecting their ability to perform at the same level they had prior to that particular injury.

This is not to say that everyone who plays sports will get hurt. My college professor once told me that there is always "an anomaly to every paradigm." This simply means that in every perceptual framework people believe in, there are always exceptions that contradict the initial statement. Patrick Maher, a philosophy teacher at Rutgers University, spoke about anomalies and paradigms in one of his lectures. He stated that,

> a paradigm became that by having unprecedented success. This is evidence that the paradigm is probably correct for the most part. Therefore an anomaly is more likely to be due to some oversight than to the falsity of the paradigm. (Maher 1962)

These facts regarding injuries and odds are not intended to scare or cause young kids to shy away from fulfilling their dreams of being the next Michael Jordan, Aaron Judge, or Tom Brady. They are simply to open up young minds to the reality that few people get the opportunity to be amongst the greatest of the great in sports. Some roadblocks and political dispositions found in sports and in life are completely out of your control. When experiencing these situations, it is important to remain resilient because there will be people, places, and things that will try to prevent you from achieving your goals.

In thinking about paradigms, norms, and values and how they affect how people view the world, I want to shift attention to a social theory described by Thomas Kuhn called "The Kuhn Cycle."

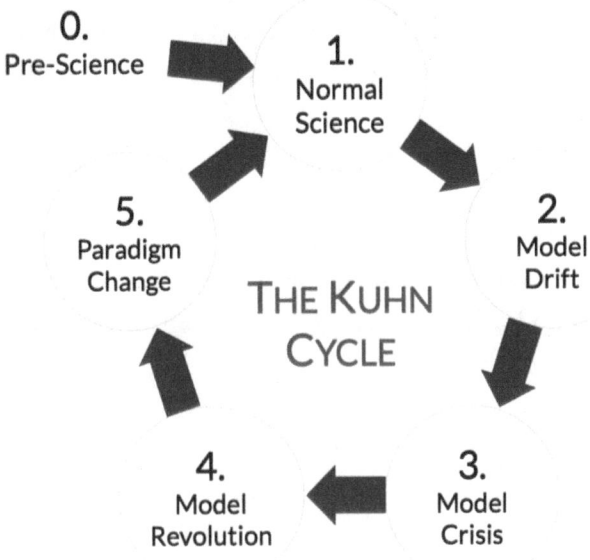

Graphic based on THOMAS S. KUHN, THE STRUCTURE OF SCIENTIFIC REVOLUTIONS (1962)

Figure 7: The Kuhn Cycle

Phase 1. Pre-science Phase.

In the pre-paradigmatic phase, the state refers to a period before a scientific consensus has been reached. There is a sense of disorganized and diverse activity. Conflict and uncertainty are high and there is no consensus.

Knowing this, I like to be very careful with the words I say and the thoughts I think. So in the pre-science phase of goal acquisition, it is important to start off with positive thoughts, beliefs, and vibrations. This creates a great foundation to help propel one to the next phase in the Kuhn Cycle.

Phase 2. Normal Science.

Normal Science lays the foundation for legitimate work within a discipline. Scientific work then consists of articulation of the paradigm, in solving puzzles that it throws up. The precedent is set in Phase 2.

Adjusting to norms in society creates opportunities for reflection where we can see what and how things come about. This also creates a chance to see how we can recreate norms and oppose structures that seem to be broken or unjust.

Phase 3. The Crisis Stage.

In the Crisis Stage, norms, routines, and rituals take a shift. Anomalies become serious, and a crisis develops if the anomalies undermine the basic assumptions of the paradigm and attempt to remove them from consistency.

I've seen this example time and time again. Where there is a transition of leadership, administration, and power of duty. In this stage, envy starts to foreshadow dissension and disengagement. Understanding this part of the curve and taking a proactive stance toward redirecting the sway of energy becomes vital. Times change, people change, but the core of who you really are and what principles you stand for should never dissipate.

Phase 4. The Revolution Stage.

In the final stage of Kuhn's Cycle, there is a new paradigm. A new sheriff is in town, so to speak. In this phase, sociological and psychological choices are exposed and identified. Contrary paradigms are considered to be incommensurable—in other words, eventually, the cream always rises to the top.

Phase 5. Paradigm Shift.

Once a single new paradigm is settled on by a few influential supporters, the Paradigm Change step begins. Here the field transitions from the old to the new paradigm while improving the new paradigm to maturity. Eventually, the old paradigm is sufficiently replaced and becomes the field's new Normal Science. The cycle then begins all over again, because our knowledge about the world is never complete.

In sports, this shift is often noticed when a new coach or new director takes over a program. A percentage of the old regime will comply with the new standards. Then you will have those that oppose change but in time, you will begin to see the beliefs and values of all parties within the organization accept what is identified as the "new normal."

CHAPTER 3

Injuries to the Body and Mind

A fitness professional would define injury as physical harm or damage to someone's body caused by an accident or an attack. I suppose injuries can result from a particular harm or damage caused by others or yourself through overuse, impact, and strenuous performance levels of intensity. In sports, these injuries seem inevitable. The intensity of physical impact can alter the amount of trauma one experiences. Physical injuries are the most commonly recognized. They can be spotted with the naked eye, which makes them easier to diagnose.

The good old-fashioned acronym of RICE seems to be the remedy to heal most fractures, bruises, and bangs. Physical therapy is the most commonly used strategy when trying to rehabilitate an injured body part. But what about those unidentified injuries? The ones that aren't reported or properly diagnosed? Somewhere out there lies a child who may not have access to the proper medical care. Furthermore, athletes who are sometimes used, abused, and exploited for their talent, sacrifice their bodies game in and game out for a team, or a school that may not care much about them. It is in circumstances like this when you may wonder, what happens to the "have-nots" in college sports? The ones that don't "make it" to the next level. That percentage represents a great number of former athletes that may potentially be suffering from mental traumas that linger from their playing days. Indeed, the most crucial undermining injuries manifest themselves in your mind.

A survey recorded in 2022, reported 38 percent of women and 22 percent of men suffered from anxiety, stress, or other forms of poor mental health. Many athletes who perform at the highest levels of competition have to confide in a certified therapist after they have played their last game. Some mental issues get resolved in time but most of them don't. How could one expect to play out their innermost potential if their mind ain't right? The answer to this is simple. One cannot compete at the highest level of play if the body and mind are not synchronized as one ego flow.

At Rutgers, we had a team therapist who would meet with us throughout the season just to check in and see how we were doing. I remember my first meeting with Dr. Charlie Maher when I was in college. We would meet with him periodically just to check in on our progress and performance on and off the court. Through the wins and all the losses for sure, we all were struggling to manage the pressure and heavy weight that is being held on our shoulders.

The "Division 1" student athlete experience is like no other individual can undergo in a lifetime. You will have some negative experiences as a student athlete as well as many positive ones. This field of experiences equipped individuals with knowledge and many other assets that prepare us for life in the real world.

Another reason why *When The Air Comes Out of the Ball* is indispensable is because, eventually after years of body trauma to your bones, the muscles will begin to deteriorate and affect your physiology and performance capability. When I reminisce about those training room talks with the guys, I can just see us tired, battered, and berated in the training room as our body parts ache. In times like these, you realize that sometimes ice, painkillers, and marijuana just isn't enough remedy to mask the pain.

On the other hand, let's look at the bright side of things. Focus on amazing, unhuman-like specimens like Lebron James or Zion Williamson. Wow! If elite performance could be displayed as a scientific formula to determine the most integral attributes found in the best players, I believe the equation would look something like this . . .

God-given ability (strength, vertical jump, flexibility, mobility, and durability) times hard work, times energy in motion (kinetic intensity) equals supreme athleticism.

Ability	**Force**	**Elite**
Power	Kinetics	**Performance**

The more injuries, bumps, and bruises one attains through physical contact, the harder it becomes to perform on a daily basis. Essentially, we are all "ticking timebombs," if you think about it. Many careers have been compromised as a direct result of physical injury.

Before the invention of microscopic surgery, a simple bump or bruise like twisted ankles, pulled groins, and torn tendons could be the beginning of the end of an athlete's career. Technology and innovations in sports medicine have reduced the rehabilitation time after injury and enhanced the body's ability to recover fast.

The exact number of careers that have been shortened due to physical injury will always be a mystery. The media tends not to publicize these situations. Actually, they disguise it pretty well. Sure you'll see a Lebron James commercial advertising sneakers or a Michael Jordan commercial for Ball Park Franks, but you'll never see an advertisement that educates consumers on the tens of thousands of injuries caused by participation in these sports and ways to recover from these injuries. It is human nature for people to seek the favorable and deny the unfavorable. One of the purposes of this chapter is to educate today's youth on some of the disadvantages of sports participation, and how to prevent these injuries from happening or keeping you off the playing field.

I am a firm believer that it is just as important for people to understand the downsides of things as it is to see the glitz and the glamour. In some cases, injuries attained through the duration of a long career can last a lifetime.

Indeed, far after your health insurance has run out with the ball club you were playing for, it is possible that those same nicks and bruises your body acquired during competition will wake up and go to sleep with you every day for the rest of your life. These injuries are problems that athletes must deal with far after the air comes out of the ball.

My father once again was an All-American football player at the University of Maryland, and he played in the National Football League for the San Francisco 49ers. He would always speak about his career-ending shoulder injury which he suffered over thirty years ago. The Maryland record books may not have many memories of this six-foot-five, 285-pound defensive end who ran the forty-yard dash in 4.8 seconds, but his injuries sustained as a football player still affected him until the day he died. He told me once when I was little, that every time it rains outside or the weather is bad, he can feel a subtle ache in his shoulder.

Can you imagine getting hurt in your twenties, and still feeling the sensation from the injury when you're in your fifties? Yes, athletics is a game. A game to be played with passion and fun. I beg young athletes who are reading this to understand that if you make a career out of any sport, you may face injury and you may possibly experience pain in the future. I recommend that you stay mentally strong and keep your eye on the prize. That prize signifies the reason for your participation. We play to be successful. We play to represent ourselves, our schools, and our families. But most of all, we play to win.

My intent in disclosing this information about injuries is not to put fear in young athletes' hearts or shame on professional sports. The purpose is, to provide a clearer understanding to those who would otherwise be ignorant of the causes and effects of injuries to the body and mind that are obtained while playing sports.

It is my belief that basketball and all other sports should be played with a tremendous amount of passion, and pride; however, it must be noted that when individuals can foresee negative trials they must go through prior to their actual occurrence, the process of persevering through them becomes easier. I can still remember my first injury during my freshman season at Rutgers University. To the public, my injury occurred in the game against our archrivals, Seton Hall University. In actuality, my injury occurred two days prior to the game when I was in practice. After limping off the court in agony from a kick to my right leg at practice, I realized that this was no ordinary minor bone bruise. I specifically remember telling one of the trainers that I could not play in our next game because of the tenderness I felt in my right leg. His response to my plea was, "Stop being soft and keep playing."

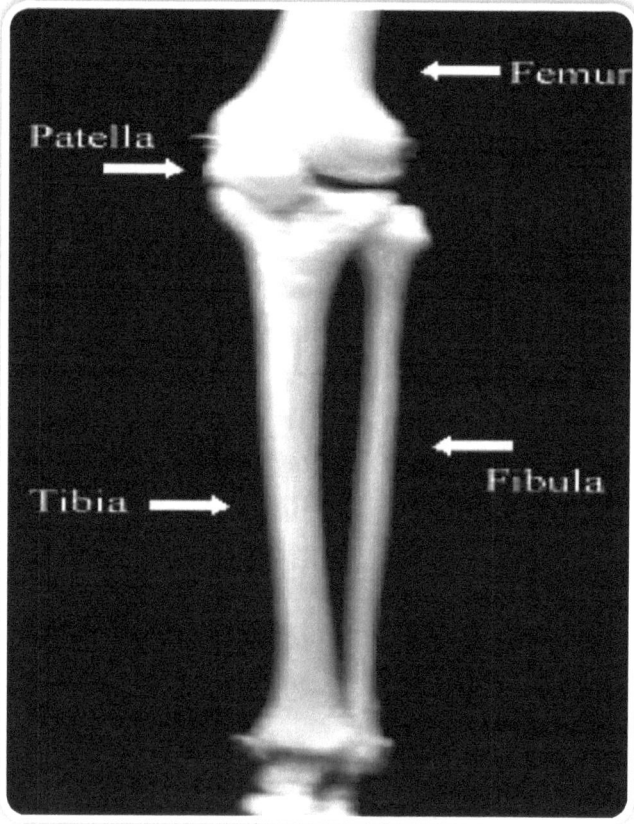

Figure 8: Picture of the skeletal bone structure of a leg. I was forced to play with a severely bruised fibula, which in turn broke as a result of constant overuse and pressure.

That wasn't necessarily what I wanted to hear after limping through a two-and-a-half-hour practice. It was resilience that allowed me to temporarily mask out the pain and distraction as I suited up the next day for the game.

I remember being at the scores table next to my teammate Anthony Farmer. As I kneeled at the scores table waiting to check in, I said, "Woogie! My legs don't feel right." Shortly after I substituted into the game, I took three or four steps to set a screen for Quincy Douby and *crack!* I fell straight to the ground screaming in pain.

I went to get an MRI to check on the "crack" that I described to the doctor after the game. The results came back that I suffered from a fractured fibula, and had to sit out for six to eight weeks. Not only did I suffer from an injury that could have been avoided, but I was rushed back to practice two weeks before I was even cleared to start my rehab. The desire to compete and the will to win made rushing back to the court convincingly tempting! Boom, Bam. Here is another lesson—when your body starts talking to you, you better listen!

From that day forward, I told myself that if I ever coached a team or trained players, I would put their health conditions first. I vowed to never force any player to play against their will.

It's hard for me not to come off as a sourpuss on this topic, but I will refrain from writing controversial statements that can be perceived as being transparently demeaning.

Discernment is an essential character trait that some would consider implicit and God-given. When I learned this method of psychology, it enabled me to anticipate misconceptions and face obstacles that can be detrimental to my well-being. Throughout my respectable basketball career, I was exposed to the glitz and glamour as well as the whips and scorns. Through it all, I can honestly say that at the end of the day, I believe that God was and always will be with me every day. Day in and day out!

So, never hesitate. Eliminate doubt from your mind. Trust your instincts and pay attention to the remarks found in your inner self. If it doesn't feel right, then . . . it's not right! Athletes should never play sports with a fear of getting hurt. When you play with a negative vibration of fear, the chances of you getting hurt are at their highest peak. To further declare this concept of living without fear, I will focus on the law of attraction and how it affects your psyche.

> People's thoughts (both conscious and unconscious) dictate the reality of their lives, whether or not they're aware of it or not. Essentially, "if you really want something and truly believe it's possible, you'll get it," but putting a lot of attention and thought onto something you don't want means you'll probably get that too. (http://en.wikipedia.org/wiki/The_Law_of_Attraction)

Having an injury-free mindset is the safest way to play because it erases negative behaviors that may cause physical incidents. When you're out on the field, rink, mat, or court, don't even think "what if" or "I can't do this because of that." There isn't much you can do to prevent an injury from happening besides demonstrating proper technique at all times and wearing protective gear to assure your safety. By the time you have reached the collegiate level, you would have gained the experience to know your body's limitations. Young athletes must learn to follow their conscience, thus making more favorable decisions.

To all athletes around the world reading this section right now, I encourage you! Follow your heart! If you ever question whether your body is undergoing too much stress, simply look in the mirror, and be honest with the person you see. The most accurate evaluator in determining a person's sincerity and honesty is the reflection of the individual in the mirror—yourself.

The majority of this chapter has been focused on physical injuries. Now, I will explore the mental injuries many athletes go through that are sometimes even more threatening. Your mind is like a treasure box. If you do not protect the treasures that lie inside, they are liable to get tampered with, seized, confiscated, and otherwise compromised.

Your inner thoughts direct and lead your outer actions. This is why it is important to have positive vibrations during all practice and game competitions. If you do not have positive thoughts, your performance will be negatively affected.

There is a great psychosocial theory called the "Law of Vibration" that indicates why it is important to control your inner thoughts and how they impact the decisions you make. The law of vibration as explained by Bob Proctor means this,

"When your subconscious mind, which is also your emotional mind, has a different belief system than what you are wishing for, your beliefs will win because they are thousands of times stronger than your desires."

So if you want a new house and start a new business, it won't happen if the voice in your head is saying, *"Money doesn't grow on trees."*

But where does that naysaying voice come from? Why do you believe that you can't have those things?

The fact is, you've been conditioned from birth to believe that the universe operates in a very different way from what Bob and other masters of universal laws teach. You've been taught to think, in a way that moves you AWAY from things you really want.

It's not just you. We've all been conditioned this way. Children all over the world are getting this conditioning from their parents and in their classrooms right now.

But now you can learn a new way. A way that is guaranteed to bring you everything you want and more. Not because Bob and I say so. Not even because that's what has happened to us and to countless others. But because that's the way God designed the Universe" (Bob Proctor, Law of Vibration).

In today's world, athletes are publicized as some of the world's most impactful leaders as their status is admired by many. Every child wants to become the next Michael Jordan, Steph Curry, or Cristiano Ronaldo. Well, not every child, but you kinda get the gist of what I'm saying. For this reason, it is important for young athletes/players to form a positive narrative that molds their reputation. You start building your reputation as an athlete from the moment you are first scouted and recognized. Building a positive reputation will give you the support of the general public, and the instincts necessary to create meaningful impressions with future employers that may provide opportunities for you in the future.

On the other hand, negative reputations can stick with you as well. Sometimes negative reputations are formed as a direct result of previous actions. The misconception of negative reputations sometimes results from mockery, envious overshadowing, and other forms of slander and political propaganda. This stigma sometimes occurs in situations where there is no primary beneficiary of the backlash to those who formulate your public opinion.

The Pygmalion Effect is a social scientific theory that underlines the principles of reputation building. With your reputation comes expectations for how you are perceived to perform by others. As studied by social psychologists, Rosenthal and Jacobson, using elementary school students as subjects, the Pygmalion Effect can give unfair advantages to some, and disadvantages to others. It refers to,

> situations in which students perform better than other students simply because they are expected to do so. Rosenthal & Jacobson (1968/1992) report and discuss the Pygmalion effect at length. In their study, they showed that if teachers were led to expect enhanced performance from some children, then the children did indeed show that enhancement. In some cases, such improvement was about twice as much as what was shown by other children in the same class. (http://psychology.wikia.com/wiki/Pygmalion_effect)

It is important to understand the concepts of this study, as it applies to athletics and performance. With today's media having a huge effect on athletes and how they are perceived by the general public, one of the biggest issues and concerns in sports is the development of your reputation.

Willie Alfonzo (chaplain, New York Mets and New York Knicks), came to speak to my team one day after practice. I'll never forget the day when he spoke to us saying, "Guard your name, man. Guard your Name." His message was, "a call to action!" His thoughts helped me understand the importance of maintaining a positive self-image. He also encouraged us to never allow others around us to mold our image or portray us in a negative light.

I still feel as if he was speaking directly to me. At the time he came to speak to us, it was no secret that there was an uncanny relationship between some of the players and members of the coaching staff. Derogatory statements were said behind closed doors that made us appear to be incompetent and unproductive. Willie Alfonzo changed my perception of life. I am thankful for his message, as well as all the other speakers who came to Rutgers, to motivate and educate my teammates during my time "on the banks of the Old Raritan."

Correlating to the Pygmalion Effect, student athletes who have positive reputations have been proven to be more successful at their sport. I'm talking about the type of player that is always in the news, doing something positive for his community. When people expect you to be a great player, the actions you display during competition should match your perceived persona off the playing fields. In reality, we are expected to succeed, and we will, because we are Division 1 athletes. Well, a small portion of us, I suppose (lol). This is just the mindset we have. That's just the toughness we've built.

It is in our nature as human beings to be great, but most of us fail to realize just how to fully develop our innermost potential. When you don't guard your name, your reputation could be tampered with for a number of reasons—this too is a reflection of the Pygmalion Effect. When people expect less of us, it comes as no surprise when we fail. Athletes who are perceived as being a "cancer," can be ostracized, and with no one on the other side to cultivate them, they then can slip into deep layers of depression and emotional instability which together is a dangerous combination.

The mental side of sports is always the most overlooked. People just don't understand how important it is. I admit, when I was younger I underestimated the mental side of sports. As an experienced athlete, I will be the first to tell you that, if you aren't mentally sound in any sport, you cannot succeed. Poise, self-control, and self-confidence are the most important things in sports for mentally preparing yourself to succeed.

John Wooden talks about these key concepts in his books.

> Poise is one of the hardest concepts to apply to your thought process. Simply put, poise is just being you or not acting, faking, or pretending. Not trying to be something you're not, nor attempting to live up to others' expectations. Therefore, when we are being who we really are we'll have a greater likelihood of functioning nearer our own level of competency. (Wooden and Carty 2009, 82)

This concept nullifies the Pygmalion Effect, because it doesn't allow outside influences to affect your personal productivity. As an athlete, the more you focus on your talents and abilities, and less on what people think you can perform better, you'll have the chance to reach your personal altitude of satisfaction.

Self-control is similar to poise, in that it involves how you train your mind to think and react to others. Wooden defines self-control as, "the ability to discipline and keep our emotions under control" (Wooden and Carty 2009, 54). Many people have the ability to do things but they lack the discipline. Maintaining mental stability is a disciplinary procedure. You must train your mind over time to concentrate on the task at hand. Furthermore, a key ingredient of self-control is controlling your emotions. After all, "a lack of self-control not only hinders individual achievement, but it also inhibits team accomplishment" (Wooden and Carty 2009, 54). Many sports are team-oriented organizations.

When we fail to control ourselves, our judgment and common sense are affected.

Once we have learned to demonstrate self-control, we must develop confidence. Confidence to me means, the belief in one's talents and abilities which serves to mentally prepare oneself or others to become successful. In addition to my definition as well as John Wooden's belief, this is, "when we are as prepared and possess the tools to handle most of the unknowns that may come our way. We are then capable of going into an event, job, meeting, show, or any other venue with total confidence" (Wooden and Carty 2009, 86). All of these concepts together, aid the psyche in the ability to function efficiently.

When you think of all John Wooden talks about confidence, poise, etc., you start to wonder how these mental concepts can be cultivated. The truth is, most of them cannot. People are born with certain personality traits, and most mental depictions marinate in your brain. That's not to say that outside influences cannot manipulate how we think or act. Keep in mind that the way others think about us forms a subjective reality, but a subjective reality is still a reality. When you speak about reputation building, the Pygmalion Effect, and poise, all of these things go hand in hand. As an athlete, the idea of reality corresponding with our personal actuality makes us ecstatic. It is a rare occurrence when people view us as we view ourselves.

To sum it up, stay true to yourself. Develop your own sense of who you are and what you can do. The only thing you can control is what you do. Keep the focus on yourself. Stay true in whatever you do. People say things in an attempt to defame your character but when you look in the mirror and you see confidence, poise, and self-control, then others will see it too.

CHAPTER 4

Climbing Over the Hill

There comes a time in all of our lives when the path to success seems narrow, and the end of our journeys seems obscure. When these events happen, we must understand what accomplishment really means. Ask anyone who has reached any level of successful achievement, and they will tell you that during their plight to the top they first had to endure great struggle. In fact, God allows all of his living creatures to experience tribulation which prepares you for liberation.

It is in the nature of man to fall on his knees, but it is also in the nature of man to rise up out of tyranny and become an example for those who follow a similar path in the future. We are all bridge builders for future generations. The example we set in today's world will be reflected on the lives of the youth of tomorrow. Therefore, it is our social responsibility to raise the bar of ambition toward striving to be the best we can be. There is a poem written by Will Allen Dromgold, that exemplifies the importance of providing a framework of social responsibility.

The Bridge Builders

"An old man going a lone highway,
Came, at the evening, cold and gray,
To a chasm vast, and deep, and wide,
Through which was flowing a sullen tide.
The old man crossed in the twilight dim,
The sullen stream had no fear for him;
But he turned when safe on the other side,
And built a bridge to span the tide.

Old man, said a fellow pilgrim near,
You are wasting strength with building here;
Your journey will end with the ending day;
You never again will pass this way;
You've crossed the chasm, deep and wide—
Why build you this bridge at the evening tide?"

The builder lifted his old gray head:
Good friend, in the path I have come,
There followeth after me today,
A youth, whose feet must pass this way.
This chasm, that has been naught to me,
To that fair-haired youth may a pitfall be.
He, too, must cross in the twilight dim;
Good friend, I am building,
   this bridge for him."

This poem speaks to my heart, as it gives insight to the importance of hard work and developing an ambitious mindset. You should work hard for self-gratification, but the real glory of hard work comes when you lay a foundation that others can learn from and adapt into their lives.

I have my own personal experiences and obstacles that I had to overcome as we all do. I always tell myself not to let negativity affect my personal production, although this can be very challenging, especially in instances when you're dealing with people who have legitimate power over the direction of your fate. It is cowardly not to attempt to fight through adversity. Fighting gives you fuel to keep striving toward the acquisition of your dreams. Ambition is what got me through my most obscure circumstances, from the start of my career when I was young until this very day at this point of my life. I have faced falsified allegations that nearly kept me from maximizing my potential, not only as a basketball player but as a positive role model for our stars of tomorrow. Through all of this negativity, I used every fallacy as a learning experience to help better myself as an individual. Coach John Wooden explained the importance of this kind of learning in his book *Wooden:*

A Lifetime of Observations

[One should] always be learning, acquiring knowledge, and seeking wisdom with a sense that you are immortal, and that you will need much knowledge, and wisdom for that long journey ahead. Know that when you are through learning, you are through." (Wooden 1997, 30)

As long as your brain is functioning, you should make it a point each and every day to learn something new. I challenge all my readers each day to learn one thing new whether it is about yourself or about others. There is only one way to move past any mistake you may make, and that is to educate yourself about the errors you've made and take the necessary steps toward correcting those errors.

A word that will further help you understand the importance of hard work is *diligence,* the persistence and hard-working effort to achieve a goal. Consistently working hard to complete a task is diligence in a nutshell. Athletes should push themselves without becoming, "fake hustlers," people who only display a work ethic when coaches or other people are watching them work. This may put you temporarily in the forefront in the eyes of your spectators but in the long run, you're hoodwinking your viewers and cheating yourself.

Coach Wooden also believed that, "things are directed in some sort of way, and that they always turn out best for those who make the best of the way things turn out" (Wooden 1997, 42). Life won't always be a "crystal stair." When the journey seems improbable and the going gets tough, I challenge you to climb over that hill. God has created us to be strong thriving creatures. Use His natural gifts toward helping you defeat your enemies and those who despise you. You will come to find in life that there are so many who want to build up the weak by tearing down the strong. Don't let the "naysayers" control the outcome of your life. Consider yourself a captain commanding his or her own ship. You control the sails and which way you will steer yourself—no one else. Diligent leaders develop ways to displace negativity. When dealing with adversity, if you can wake up in the morning, look yourself in the mirror, and say that you refuse to give up, then you have established the concept of diligence.

When the going gets tough ask yourself these questions: Am I prepared to weather the storm? Can I manage to perform, although elite performance seems highly unlikely? If the answer to these questions is yes, you have just demonstrated determination. Determination can be defined as, "the process of deciding on or establishing a course of action" (Dictionary.com). God has many blessings in store for all of us. These blessings however are not free. After all, nothing in life is free. God asks us to stay motivated and strive toward perfection, and this is when he delivers and you receive your reward. Don't take shortcuts. When we cheat our way through life, we are only cheating ourselves. If no one else respects us, we must respect ourselves. "Set your compass in a chosen direction and then focus your attention and efforts completely on the journey of preparation. A successful journey becomes your destination, and is where your real accomplishment lies"

(Wooden, 54). Give yourself credit for attempting to do something that others can't or refuse to do.

A key point in developing determination is creating goals for yourself. A goal is a by-product of all the hard work and good thinking you do along the way. It is your own personal preparation where success is truly found. Don't measure success by whether you won a game or earned an award. Measure your success by whether you gave it your best. Even if you have given your best, there is a chance that you may not get lucky. Keep in mind that luck is when preparation meets opportunity. On the flip side of this phrase, understand that failing to prepare is preparing to fail. If you take the proper steps to be ready for whatever shall come your way, you are indirectly controlling your own fate.

After you have embraced the concept of hard work and determination, it is now your responsibility to practice what you preach. Put all of the values you've learned throughout your life to proper use. This concept can be exceptionally hard for collegiate student athletes. The responsibilities of being an educated sportsman/sportswoman are often taken for granted. For those who have never had the experience of shining as a superior athlete on the college level, they may not be aware of the responsibility pressures we may face. Superstars who shy away from the responsibility that comes with public acclaim don't have a choice in the matter. They are role models whether they like it or not, and they cannot simply announce that they intend to relinquish their social responsibility.

It should be a goal of all college and professional athletes to become good role models. When you are in the public eye, you should be very conscious of your actions. Everyone is watching you, and most people want you to do something negative so they can take a screenshot and post it on social media the next day. Do not misconstrue what I am saying here. I am not saying that to be a good role model you have to live a perfect life. In fact, some of the best role models live the most imperfect lives, but they are accountable for their actions. That is what makes them great leaders.

> You can make mistakes, but you aren't a failure until you start blaming others for those mistakes. When you blame others, you are trying to excuse yourself. When you make excuses, you can't properly evaluate yourself. Without proper self-evaluation, failure is inevitable. (Wooden, 56)

This is possibly the hardest thing athletes have to deal with in the public eye. No one wants to be perceived as a failure or a screwup. When people do not live up to their own standards or those of others around them, it is only natural to feel embarrassed. Rather than spending time on the errors you make, focus on improvements you can implement to make yourself more efficient the next go around. Coach Wooden once said with regard to his players, "I feel that hard public criticism antagonizes them, and may discourage them from being receptive to a message. It is counterproductive, whether it's on a basketball court or in a business establishment" (Wooden, 118). It takes a brave person to come out of their comfort zone and do things that may embarrass them. Realize that bravery nullifies embarrassment. The more willing you are to do something, the less embarrassed you should feel if things don't turn out the way you anticipated them to.

Sometimes we reach points in our life when we feel like things just haven't been going our way. I admit that I have reached certain points in my life when I have felt like I was getting the short end of the stick. Sometimes you just want to start over or renew your enthusiasm for a particular matter. The Bible speaks of an apostle named Paul. This man was not happy with how he was living his life and thus changed his name from King Saul to Paul the Apostle. This change represented a new beginning for how he was going to live his life. This was Paul's way of repenting to God and displaying spiritual rehabilitation. Similar to how Paul changed his self-image, I too decided to change the narrative of who people thought I was. I wanted to show the world what I was capable of, and my, oh my was I excited as ever to manifest my own destiny! It was time for the world to meet the real "JR Inman."

This restoration of perspective was my personal attempt to show people who I really am, contrary to erroneous belief. To me, coming into my own, represented a maturation process. I have risen above and beyond all negative scrutiny and now have transcended into a new lifestyle and way of thinking. I continue to develop a plan to further solidify myself as a metropolitan basketball icon because it is my belief that this is my social responsibility. "God has a plan for each of us that will enable us to be all that he created us to be" (Wooden and Carty 2009, 34).

I strive on a daily basis to perform formidable actions that are in accordance with God's plans, goodwill, and mercy. The key to executing any plan is patience. Sometimes people have the, "I want it now" attitude. Hastiness is a primary reason why people don't get the results they expect. Please don't confuse patience with laziness. Just because things may not happen immediately doesn't give us a reason to procrastinate. Strive to act in situations as if the deadline is tomorrow. If you prepare for tomorrow today, then when tomorrow comes, you will be prepared today!

When you think you have given it your all, you probably have not. There is no substitute for hard work. "If we put out minimum effort, we may get by in some situations, but in the long run we won't fully develop the talents that lie within us" (Wooden and Carty 2009, 30). It is our duty as God's children, to use all the God-given intangibles he has blessed us with. Wasting blessings is possibly the worst sin anyone could do to themselves. There are so many people in this world who would die to be in your position. Be thankful for the gifts you have been given, and work hard toward mastering them.

All God wants us to do is to live fruitfully, and just live and strive to become better people today than we were yesterday. If each day we become better people than we were the day before, we are taking yet another striding step toward climbing over the hill.

CHAPTER 5

AA Counseling
(Athletics and Academics)

Since athletics has become a mainstream sector of the educational system, one of the biggest problems our administrators have fought to correct is developing strategies that would help student athletes recognize the importance of balancing athletics with academics. Kids are so quick to pick up a ball early in the morning and head out to the courts for games of pick up lasting throughout the day, but not as quick to lock themselves in a library, to put work into preparing for the SATs or any test they may have to take.

Many elite student athletes are ready to catch a touchdown pass under pressure, or juke past their defender with the puck, but are not ready to go to study hall or endure a late-night cram session in preparation for their final exam. Why is this? In its simplest sense, what you see is what you get. In today's society, the media glorifies athletes for their accomplishments on the field but is slow to publicize their efforts in the classroom. Advertisements are often seen of professional athletes modeling a sneaker that gives them better performance on the court, rather than a notebook that can be used to memorize plays or write down notes in school. I'm not blaming this educational epidemic on the media, all I'm saying is that media advertisements play vital roles in how people view athletic performance. If game performance is the only perk advertised in being a professional athlete, then game performance is what our youth will focus on.

I challenge coaches and players to be motivated toward helping our youth understand at a young age, why it is just as important, if not more important, to be an All-American in the classroom than on the court.

Thabiti "Showtime" Boone, a native of Brooklyn, and a New York streetball legend wrote a book titled *Rising to the Occasion*. This book focuses on the magnitude of complementing your "in game" performance with your "in classroom" performance. Here Thabiti writes,

> Understanding the importance, and connection between sports, and academics gave me a new meaning in my approach to playing ball. I began to learn that sports and academics meant I was playing for my future so I had to study hard to make the grade. (p. 62)

The future is what we should be preparing for. After all the past is gone and will never come again, and what you do right now, in the present, will affect how you live your life in the future. Make preparations today for tomorrow's happenings. You don't have to be a straight A student. Lord knows my report card was always far from perfect. I always focused on the importance of trying as hard as I could to make sure that I excelled academically. My parents used to always encourage me to "make the grade" in the classroom. I never understood why they were so adamant about me doing the best I could do in the classroom, but I later realized that without knowledge you have nothing.

My mother used to always say to me that "knowledge is power." She firmly believed that equipping yourself with all the knowledge you can will prepare you to be an asset to society. This enabled me to value my education at an early age. Performing in the classroom simply means reaching the maximum of your scholastic capabilities. Not everyone can be an A student across the board. Not everyone will make the dean's list or even get a full academic scholarship to college, but everyone can excel in the classroom by working hard to reach their personal ideal of success. Academic prosperity comes from within. Realizing your intellectual potential is the first step toward creating a goal that when fulfilled will give you a sense of academic achievement.

My parents encouraged me to make the honor roll every marking period when I was in high school, and rightfully so—they were paying thousands of dollars a year to invest in an education that would put me on a level with other premier high school scholars and peers. For my parents, making the honor roll was a symbol of the hard work that I had put into my academics during the marking period. I would always fall one or two As short of qualifying for the honor roll, but I know that I worked hard to be the best student I could be, and that made me feel successful within myself. Was I a straight A student across the board during all of my years in high school and college? No, but did I devote time each and every day toward maintaining a desirable academic standard? The answer is most certainly yes!

Jason McCourty, my childhood basketball teammate and retired professional cornerback for the Tennessee Titans, described to me what the importance of balancing athletics and academics always meant to him and his brother Devin,

> I never had an option when it came to doing well in the classroom. From the beginning, my mother made sure that my grades were at least an A or B before I took part in any sport. I've learned that athletics can be taken from you at any time, whether through an injury or just being told you can't do it. At some point, it will come to an end. What you learn in the classroom is something that will stay with you your entire life.

It's no wonder Jason and his brother Devin each have solidified their position on the Mount Rushmore of NFL brothers, not only with their amazing athletic abilities but also their character. Excelling in academics gives you a platform to demonstrate your character, and that is what

Jason worked hard for in his days as a student athlete. Even today, as he continues to strive toward solidifying himself as a premier defensive back in the NFL, he still carries his values with him.

In the previous chapter, "Climbing over the Hill," I spoke of the value of work ethic and its relevance in persevering through adverse situations. I look at AA counseling like a sandwich. Academics and athletics are the slices of bread. Success is the turkey and cheese, and work ethic is the condiment that makes the sandwich taste good.

Comparatively, if you demonstrate work ethic in the classroom, the energy and values used here can transcend into your approach on the playing field and on the basketball court. "The power of sports and academics is the understanding that they are inseparable, and are equally important from the standpoint of how they both feed off each other" (Boone 2000). Think about how much time you spend each day on developing your body for elite performance. This includes weight training, forming a good diet, practicing, watching a film, or analyzing your opponent. Now think of the amount of time you spend daily strengthening your mind. This includes studying, doing extra credit, reviewing notes, and getting proper rest so you can be sharp and attentive in class. I think that if the average athlete does this comparison, they will come to find that they spend much more time preparing for game competitions than they do in their preparation for the classroom.

What will replace the time you devote toward your athletic capabilities when your playing career has come to a halt? These are questions many young athletes should think about now rather than later. "It's amazing how so many athletes blow their opportunities to further advance their education and playing careers. It's like having a winning lottery ticket and you don't turn it in to claim your prize" (Boone 2000).

Why invest time in becoming a great athlete or a great student and then not fulfill the ultimate goal of AA superiority? It sickens my stomach to think of the number of professional basketball players that never got an opportunity to play professional basketball. Sometimes we hold ourselves back from being great athletes and great students. Fear, ignorance, lack of preparation, and poor judgment are some of the things we allow to get in our way of success.

Understand that the time you put into your academics and athletics are investments from which you receive a lifetime of returns. Life can sometimes be seen as a practical trade-off. "If you give school your hard work and dedication, then you owe it to yourself to work hard and dedicate yourself towards receiving your degree" (Boone 2000).

In some cases, young student athletes may not know how to focus their intelligence toward a specific field of study. In these situations, I would advise a young athlete to work hard in all subject areas until you find your niche or something you think you may prosper in. I went into college thinking I was going to major in finance. It wasn't until my junior year in college that I realized I had a passion for writing and information processing. It was then that I declared my major and started writing this book. This book has a unique message. It speaks of life after sports, although my career is far from over. It is my solemn belief that I am making preparations for the day my playing days are no more. I like to think of myself as an intelligent student athlete who graduated from a first-class academic institution.

I don't measure my self-worth by wins, losses, or the number of points I scored in college (though it was 1,036 points). I evaluate my abilities based on the amount of knowledge I acquire and the amount of intelligence I absorb each day. At the end of the day, sports don't make us who we are, but intelligence does.

Athletes should work hard toward achieving academic excellence for pride—pride in knowing that you started working toward something (knowledge and intelligence) that produced a tangible artifact (high school diploma and college degree). Don't be selfish. The majority of athletes have people in their lives who have sacrificed or invested time toward putting them in a position to succeed.

Our parents are first and foremost on the list of people who can provide a means of excellence. Our coaches also have a vast input in our achievements. "Coaches take pride when their athletes graduate and receive their high school or college diplomas. Parents and coaches should be responsible for the future of our children; we help to shape and nurture their abilities and ambitions to be successful in life" (Boone 2000).

Figure 9: Gerald H. Inman Jr. on Graduation Day, Rutgers University Class of 2009

To my parents, family, friends, and all who ever believed in me, thank you! They say pictures can sometimes say a thousand words. Words can't express how proud I am to have the opportunity to demonstrate my appreciation toward my encouraging support system.

As long as athletes are role models and public figures, there will always be spectators who evaluate their performances and try to measure their success. Remember that success comes from within. If you can look in the mirror and honestly say to yourself that you gave it your all, then you are by all means successful. A message to all the athletes reading this book who will not make it to the pros: "Even if you fall short of your sports dreams, at least you will have learned how to channel your athletic interests into a motivational and disciplinary tool to help you reach for success in other life's aspirations and goals" (Boone 2000).

The values you receive by participating in sports correspond with the values necessary for succeeding in life. After all, sports are a big part of our lives, but they are not our lives.

It is always good to receive advice on a particular subject from different standpoints. During this chapter you have had insight from Thabiti "Showtime" Boone, who is a notorious ball court street legend; now I will share some insight from an entrepreneur by the name of Randal Pinkett. Mr. Pinkett is a Rutgers graduate and former student athlete who managed to launch a multimillion-dollar business during his time "on the banks of the Old Raritan."

After his business started to thrive, he wrote a book titled *Campus CEO*, an entrepreneurial guide to launching a successful business. In one section of his book, he explained,

> The most important lesson I learned about being a good student was to be a student of being a good student. Stated differently, I realized that if I wanted to master my studies I would have to learn the best way for me to learn, and that means addressing three areas: studying, test-taking techniques, time management, and stress management. (Pinkett, 190)

These four areas of concentration are vital in elite performance in the classroom, in sports, and in the development of a small business. Studying familiarizes your mind with topics covered during class discussion and information that can provide depth to your subject material. Test-taking is a way that professors can evaluate a student's ability to apply the information taught in class and measure their overall receptiveness. With collegiate athletes, time management becomes the ability to prioritize your schedule so that you complete each responsibility you have as a student athlete. Stress management teaches you how to develop ways to cope with the anxieties that student athletes inevitably go through during the course of a semester or season. The more time you invest in the maintenance of these four categories, the easier it will be to cope with these AA regularities.

Do not underestimate the importance of incorporating a social life into your collegiate experience. The mind is a constant, ongoing machine that only hibernates at night when you are sleeping. Rebuilding your mind with social activity is vitally important in maintaining mental focus and development. "The fact that I was a college athlete enabled me to receive regular exercise, and make no mistake, yes, I still made time to have a social life, spend time with friends, and go to parties" (Pinkett 2007). These are the words of a former student athlete who now has acquired millions of dollars through hard work and determination. The key to excellence is not boredom or isolation, it is finding a balance between the time you spend with your family and friends and the time you spend molding yourself into being as close to perfect as you can possibly become. For example, if you have a final exam on Friday, you don't go out binge drinking on Monday, clubbing on Tuesday and Wednesday, and then cram Thursday night for an exam on Friday. Also, if your team just won the national championship, it is completely unnecessary to have a midnight curfew and wake up for a 9:00 a.m. study hall the next day.

As you get older and more mature, you will learn how to make sound judgments and decisions. You will learn when it is time to party and when it's time to buckle down and focus. AA counseling is actually a skill, because the process of balancing your academics with your athletics takes practice and experience to learn. Surround yourself with people who are as focused as you are or want to be. This will make it easier for you to determine when it is appropriate to "entertain" and when it's appropriate to "enter your brain."

There is one thing that all collegiate students have in common: test-taking. Since the merging of minority and Caucasian students post-Civil Rights Era, there have been speculations that would indicate that standardized tests are culturally biased. Scientific theories have proven that from the time we are young, children from ethnic backgrounds are socialized and domestically cultured in different ways than kids who are of Caucasian descent.

This disparity is by no means an excuse for African American and Hispanic American students not to perform in the classroom. It just fortifies how important it is for kids who fall within these racial demographics to work that much harder to achieve scholastic excellence. Although this barrier exists, I do believe there are general guidelines that aid all students in reaching a desirable type of success.

Randal Pinkett outlined some test-taking strategies that are very important in a student athlete's approach before, during, and after a test is taken. The strategies are as follows:

Figure 9: Randal Pinkett's Test Strategies

Pretest Strategies

1. Create notes/flashcards you can review until the test.
2. Determine what topics lend themselves to essays.
3. Take quizzes seriously; prepare for them as you would a test. Keep in mind that the information may appear on the exam.
4. Read directions and questions carefully, paying particular attention to the number of points awarded for each question. Budget your time accordingly.
5. Save your study notes and quizzes for the final examination.

During Test Strategies

1. Write important formulas on the back of the test before you begin (where applicable).
2. Read the directions carefully! Read the entire test before you begin, and answer the easiest questions first. Budget your time.
3. Show all your work for partial credit. Do not leave any answers blank.
4. Verify that all the answers make sense. Check your answers when time permits.

Post-Test Strategies

1. Do not discuss the exam with other students immediately after it is over. You will only depress yourself.
2. When you get the exam back, analyze it thoroughly. Make sure that you understand why you missed the questions you missed and why you were correct on the ones you got right.
3. Save all exams for use in studying for the final examination.
4. Do not let old test scores paralyze you with anxiety.

All of my student athlete readers should find this portion of the book most helpful in their personal test-taking techniques. You should institute the management between balancing your academic life with your athletic life. I encourage you to stay motivated toward achieving AA excellence. If this balance has been somewhat of a struggle for you, then reading information on enhancing your time management skills, such as you'll find in this book, is the first step toward change. Remember, it's never too late to turn over a new leaf and start walking on that straight and narrow path toward success in all of life's aspirations. The experiences you go through will ultimately stick with you throughout all the days of your life, whether it be academic or athletic. Why not develop positive memories that you can share with future generations about times in your young student athlete life when you were able to defeat the odds and accomplish what so many struggle to persevere through? It is no walk in the park being a collegiate student athlete. If you have ever been a student athlete in college or knew a student athlete, then this is a fact that few will beg to differ.

    I want all of my student athletes here and now to take a vow. Vow to yourself that you will take this AA counseling section of the book most seriously. Vow that you will put equal effort, if not more, into the classroom as you put on the playing fields. If you can honestly say with a bright smile that you strove your hardest toward excellence in the classroom and during elite athletic competition, then you, my friend, have taken heed to AA counseling.

CHAPTER 6

Goals Grant Greatness

If you were given the task of creating a list of the top ten most socially admirable athletes in the history of professional sports, I guarantee you will find two commonalities: self-motivation and goal achievement. Goals provide a vision that people can strive toward. These intangible attributes are completely necessary in order to achieve competitive greatness. "Wishful thinking," is another way to describe the thought process of creating a goal for yourself and developing strategies toward the execution of these goals. If you want things to happen for you, then make them happen. Don't talk about it, be about it. Strive to always be prepared to manifest your capabilities when called upon.

If I could break down an equation for success in sports, it would look something like this:

$$\frac{Motivation \times Determination}{Inspiration \times Reputation} = \frac{Success}{Admiration}$$

Figure 10 : Inmanology Formula for Success

In its most practical sense, all of these words listed in Figure 7 are stepping stones toward success, but I must expound upon each word so you can understand its relevance to personal achievement.

1. Motivation - The process that arouses, sustains, and regulates human and animal behavior.

2. Determination - The ascertaining or fixing of the quantity, quality, position, or character of something.

3. Inspiration - An agency, such as a person or work of art that moves the intellect or emotions or prompts action or invention.

4. Reputation - The general estimation in which a person is held by the public.

5. Success - The achievement of something desired, planned, or attempted.

6. Aspiration - A strong desire for high achievement.

The culmination of the terms in the formula for success is impossible to congregate by yourself. This is why support systems are essential for your personal development. My strongest support system is my parents. Together, they have always believed in my capabilities and never doubted my talents.

The position of coach, mentor, or religious leader often requires individuals to motivate people through communication. When athletes are motivated to achieve excellence, then excellence is what we will strive toward. Basketball season is a long road ending in a narrow highway. Your support systems are designated drivers of your life. If these drivers aren't sober behind the wheel, then don't frustrate yourself if you happen to run off path. The truth is that if you step out of or away from your support systems, your reputation becomes a way for others to determine your success. Under these circumstances, I would advise someone to create a way to use the support systems you do have as an innovative method toward the self-manifestation of your inspiration.

I had the pleasure of growing up and competing against some of the most elite athletes of this millennium. I met Ray Rice (running back, Baltimore Ravens) back in our dorm room during my freshman year in the suites on Bush Campus. I knew that he was going to be a great football player. He looked like an NFL running back. Although he was an eighteen-year-old football stud still wet behind the ears, his demeanor was that of an NFL star. During his sophomore season, he reached a point when he realized how great he actually could be. Coach Schiano and fellow star fullback Brian Leonard (an NFL draft pick) provided support and inspiration that allowed Ray's potential to flourish into an "RU Lucky Charm."

Mike Rosario was brought to Rutgers to be the savior of the Rutgers University men's basketball program. Reaching a thousand points in just his sophomore season, he became the youngest thousand-point scorer in Rutgers history at nineteen years old. Since the day Mike walked into Louis Brown Athletic Center, he was handed the reins of the program. This motivated Michael and enabled him to earn freshman All-American honors and become a member of the 2008 All-Big East All-Rookie team. This personal achievement of Michael's may not have led to overall team success (26 wins–48 losses during his tenure); however, he will be remembered as an honorary member of the Rutgers University all-time thousand-point club.

Jason and Devin McCourty (NFL Pro Bowl cornerbacks, Rutgers University) have reached the absolute pinnacle of their prominence in professional sports. The twin brothers, with their charm and eloquent demeanor, have been working toward being elite athletes from the beginning of their athletic careers playing Pop Warner football.

Figure 10: 2002 Saint Joseph Regional High School Men's Basketball Team (Jason, Devin, and JR Inman)

Figure 10.1: JR Inman, Bergen County Jamboree, Winter 2002

Figure 10.2: JR Inman, SJR Alumni Basketball, Winter 2023

I remember the first day I saw Jason and Devin on the bus to school. We were thirteen years old. I had always seen them at Pilgrim Baptist Church, so their faces looked familiar. Little did either of us know that together we would compete for two county titles (2002 Freshman Bergen County Basketball Champions and 2005 Bergen County Jamboree Champions) and one state title (Parochial B State Finals vs. Seaton Hall Preparatory School).

I remember the twins being straight A students in high school and members of the National Honor Society. I always respected both of them, not only for their athletic capabilities but also for their academic achievements. Long before these fellows were catching interceptions from Hall of Fame NFL quarterbacks, I saw something special in each of them.

Their intricate synergy created a hard force to pass through on the basketball court. It was a pleasure playing basketball with them, so I wasn't surprised when I saw Dev catching picks in the Pro Bowl or Jay shutting Hall of Fame wide receivers down. Both of these men are great athletes because they prepared themselves to be great. In an interview I conducted with Devin McCourty last fall, he said,

> I always remind myself of my goals and use my goals as motivation and guidance towards making decisions. Always make decisions that will help you get closer to your goals. My Mom instilled the importance of schoolwork in me and my brother. School gave me discipline and gave me the opportunity to better myself as a person throughout my life.

This speaks volumes about the morals Devin's mother, Phyllis, instilled in her twin boys. For me, it feels good to have affiliations with guys who are doing the right thing, as Spike Lee once said.

Hamady N'Diaye's excursion to America in search of a better life from the deep jungles of Dakar, Senegal, facilitates further discussion of how one can achieve success through the fulfillment of goals.

Figure 11: JR Inman and Hamaday N'Diaye against Syracuse University (2007 Rutgers Men's Basketball Season)

Figure 11.1: Hamaday N'Diaye, Rokee, Sacramento Kings, NBA Drive, 2010

Hamaday—or H, as I call him—would often reflect on times when he was a little man walking the streets of Senegal. Well, it's hard to imagine a seven-foot shot-blocking monster ever being a little boy, but believe it or not there once was a time when Hamaday used to look up to people. Life was hard for him and his family growing up in a small village inside the city walls of a town only a few generations removed from the socioeconomic disparity that blemishes some of the hardest streets of Dakar. From the time H stepped on a plane to enter the United States of America, he had a dream to someday rise up to the heights of the National Basketball Association. He faced his own battles like learning English as a second language and playing games hurt due to an overuse injury in his back. If you ask H, he'll tell you that he never doubted that he would make it to the NBA. His determination provided a ticket to fulfill the promise he made to his family. He vowed that he would do whatever it took to make an NBA roster.

The list goes on and on of athletes I have come across who have figured out in their own ways how to achieve success in sports. Sports provides a framework of understanding for its participants on how to utilize objects within your environment and correlate them together in order to produce a functioning product. Athletes who merge into the business world after college are often efficient workers because their athletic experiences equip them with hard work and motivation to succeed at a particular task. To be great is to strive. To strive is to pursue achievement. Achievers believe in achieving. Their confidence within themselves attracts a corresponding assurance from people who are evaluating their actions. Believing is only half the battle. As I have often told my student athletes, once you have convinced yourself that you are capable of accomplishing an achievement, motivation will be the most vital ingredient in the final manifestation of your expositional identity.

Figure 12: JR Inman, League Commissioner, JCC Premiere Basketball League, Spring 2023

Figure 13: JR "throwing it down" in Kyoto, Japan vs. Okinawa (Winter 2009)

CHAPTER 7

Giving Back

The life of a collegiate student athlete requires individuals to have a keen sense of social responsibility. We are public figures and people view our actions as direct accusations that result from the social acclaim of being an athletic figure. Each of us must lead by example and convey a socially desirable reputation. For this reason, it is our duty to appreciate our support systems. These are the figures in our lives who help create our reality. Your roots are the core of all that you are today and all that you will ever be in life. Every time I leave Rockland County, New York, I pray that the Lord will bless me to return with peace, love, and prosperity.

*Figure 14: Inmanology 101 at Rocktown Basketball Academy
"Each one, teach one, grab one, reach one" (Regional Sainte-Rose).*

Instructing the youth in the Rockland/Bergen County area has become a deep passion of mine. Each child I train has their own particular attribute that needs to be renovated. I challenge them to make their weaknesses their strengths and their strengths even stronger. Time, energy, and patience are a few words that come to mind when I think of what's needed to inspire natural talent.

Sometimes adults have the tendency to forget what it's like to be young. There was a point in each of our lives when we were illiterate or incapable of functioning properly. Where would we be without the influence of our elders? They have expertise in a variety of specific topics. When I was younger, I would sometimes reprimand those who tried to help me. I didn't understand their purpose or intent. Our ancestors instituted foundations that we can choose to utilize or rebuke. These are the people in each of our lives who deserve the most credit. It is because of them that we even exist. Quite frankly, without a helping hand, we just can't make it in today's society.

I always keep this in mind when I step on the court, whether I'm training myself or training someone else who may benefit from my expertise. Our youth are our future. We have the power to change the world as we know it through our interactions with future generations. It is our duty to provide a good example for our followers by being just in our dealings and faithful in our engagements. Giving back to your community requires individuals to demonstrate leadership qualities. Leaders lead by example, but they can also be taught or instructed on how to lead.

Often in our society, we see tyrants fail to seek advice from people who fall beneath their hierarchical status. The instant we stop seeking advice from others, our leadership capabilities begin to falter. The best leaders are usually the best listeners.

We don't learn from speaking and giving instructions. Listening allows our minds to be enlightened with feedback from a secondary source. Every mind thinks differently, and each person shares a different field of experience. As you grow older, you may have the privilege of meeting many different people. Always establish networks and take something positive from individuals so you may apply it to your own life.

I take everything I've learned and try to teach someone else who may benefit from my acquisition of knowledge. My experiences, combined with the knowledge I have acquired during all of my worldly travels, have given me a unique sense of wisdom. There are many young people who are blessed with natural intellect. They are able to grasp concepts quickly, which enables them to have a shrewd perspective. Even for these particular students, it is best for them to receive instruction from an individual or superior who has proficient experience.

When the Air Comes Out of the Ball

Michael Jordan is one of the greatest players to ever walk on God's green earth. Even he was supervised and evaluated by his Coach, Phil Jackson, who is arguably the best professional basketball coach in NBA history. Jordan always led by example. Even so, he still received instruction from his superior who he recognized possessed greater basketball knowledge. Would Jordan have been as successful without the support and leadership of Hall of Fame Coach Phil Jackson? We will never know. One thing we do know is that Jordan's ability, combined with his effort, was elevated by Phil Jackson's wisdom and expertise. This produced six championships and arguably the best professional basketball team in the history of the sport.

There are many groups and organizations that you can join to lend a helping hand in providing community service. No matter where I go in life, I always remember those that were there for me before I became who I am today. I consider all those who have helped elevate my level of achievement as stepping stones. These stepping stones have brought me to a point where I can now be proud of myself, my accomplishments, and the direction in which I am going with my life.

When I came to college as an eighteen-year-old freshman, I was satisfied with my personal accomplishments. They made me feel happy, which provided me with a sense of fulfillment. During the next three years of my career, I endured the "constructive discharge" of my head basketball coach, a traumatizing knee surgery, and an overall win-loss record of thirty-three wins and ninety-two losses. These adversities flustered my mind.

Regardless of all the frustration that was going on in my life at that time, I never forgot my initial mission when I decided to sign my letter of intent to play college basketball at Rutgers University. I fought through the tough times and developed new ways to keep my mind motivated toward fulfilling my dream of earning a college degree.

During the summer of my junior year in college, I was called to become an esteemed member of the Omega Psi Phi Fraternity, Inc.

Fraternities and sororities are great collegiate organizations that uplift the community through service and nationally mandated programs.

Figure 15: JR Inman, Mark Jenkins, and Kenny Smith (Omega Psi Phi Fraternity, Inc. TZ FALL '08)

The Omega Psi Phi Fraternity Incorporated renewed my enthusiasm during my junior and senior years at Rutgers University. Whenever I felt like things just weren't going my way, I would call upon my frat brothers and they would give me an uplift. Together we developed programs that would educate our peers on the issues going on in today's world. In the first picture to the left shown in Figure 16, I, along with my line brothers Mark Jenkins and Kenny Smith, facilitated an on-campus program titled "Obama for Change." This pep rally took place during the campaign of presidential candidate Barack Obama. Our mission was to encourage all of our voters at Rutgers University to vote for Barack Obama in the upcoming election. Barack's theme for his democratic campaign was "Change." We, the brothers of Omega Psi Phi Fraternity Incorporated, LLC, were avid supporters of his regime and worked hard to gain the support of the student body at Rutgers throughout Obama's presidential campaign.

College provides a wide variety of organizations that can give you a public voice and assist in promoting prosperity and leadership within your community. Along with my initiation into Omega Psi Phi, I also decided to attend Black Student Union meetings. Black Student Unions are organizations that bring together African American students. They give minorities opportunities to express themselves by voicing their opinions on issues facing ethnic students in today's educational system. Furthermore, they provide opportunities to be proactive in developing ways to achieve excellence in higher institutions of learning.

Being a collegiate athlete was not enough for me. I felt that God wanted me to do so much more than just play sports. My determination to achieve success led me to believe that I must do anything possible for the assurance that I would have an impact on future aspiring student athletes who would one day strive to be overachievers just like I was.

Stewardship is the terminology that my mother taught me when I was younger. From time to time, she would bring me to the church on days I had off from school. She and I would help the elderly women in the church with cooking, cleaning, and church maintenance. At the time, I was too young to understand why she made me do this, especially if I wasn't getting paid. She would always tell me that God blesses those that practice stewardship.

She would encourage me and tell me that my work was not going unnoticed, that the true blessings come from above. That is why we as followers of Christ help others without the intent of receiving any direct benefit.

These principles of stewardship stayed with me into my adult life. Oftentimes when I help people, I don't even ask for money or profit. It is my duty as a follower of Christ to help all those in need. If I can be of assistance to anyone, then a simple thank you is all I need to feel gratified. The idea of giving without receiving can be a hard concept to manifest in your life. After all, as humans we are self-interested actors. The majority of our actions and interactions with others serves a purpose to further advance ourselves as individuals. In today's competitive world, it is very seldom that you shall find someone who has a genuine motive of helping others. This is why it is even more important to have a spirit of compassion and to continue to inspire others to live better lives. Have hope that your efforts will not go unnoticed. Believe that God sees all from above and is charting down all of your actions and efforts to make his world a better place. If you truly have faith in our Lord God, then this is all the assurance you need. Your salvation is your reward or profit from all the good intent you cast out while you were living. Be grateful for your abilities and use them to help motivate your successors. Take not for granted what you do have in life. This is how God wants us to act as disciples of Christ. This is how Christ has taught us to live: faithful, noble, and righteous.

The lifestyle of a professional athlete is admirable. We hold positions in society that some respect and venerate, and others envy and admonish. Rather than focus on the negative, ill-mannered critics in our harsh world, I gravitate toward those who show appreciation for my duties. In most cases, I find this adoration in the youthful community. There is something special about children that is admirable. An adolescent mind has not yet been exposed to extreme levels of scrutiny, deceit, pain, and agony; therefore their thoughts are pure, just, and filled with good intent in most cases.

Sports has given me tools to speak, educate, and inform many kids from different cultures. Throughout my travels, I have seen millions of faces and been exposed to many different backgrounds. Of my many experiences, I will reflect on one that can never be forgotten.

It was another day of basketball practice in Fukuoka, Japan. I was beginning my preparation for the upcoming 2011–2012 basketball season. We had a seventh grade boys' basketball team come to our practice to experience what it was like to be inside a professional basketball practice. None of the boys on the team spoke good English, but I saw that they all had the same problem. When they were passing the balls to each, they were not using the proper technique. I was working out with one of my teammates, Kevin Palmer (Washington Wizards shooting guard), when I saw that they were making erroneous

When the Air Comes Out of the Ball

passes. Afterward, I walked over to our team translator and asked him to grab one of the boys' attention and translate a message for him.

I told him, "Always fake the direction of the pass you want to throw the ball. If you want to throw a chest pass, fake the bounce pass first, then throw it. If you want to throw a bounce pass, fake the chest pass first, then throw it."

The translator told the young boy my message and the boy began throwing the ball to me the correct way. I had him feed me over one hundred times to ensure that this lesson would marinate in his basketball brain. At the end of the drill, I was about to walk off and change my clothes and go home. The translator grabbed me and said, "JR, the boy has something to say to you." I turned to the boy, and he smiled at me and said, "Good job."

I remembered feeling so good that day not because of the job I did, but because basketball enabled me to break a language barrier and have an impact on someone's life. That boy will always remember me as the professional ballplayer that showed him how to pass a basketball. I have played basketball for many years and can probably count the number of coaches, fans, or critics on one hand that has ever told me that I did a "good job." We sometimes underestimate the power of positive opinions. That little boy knew little to no English. He barely even knew my name, yet he impacted my self-esteem more than many other people who I've come across during my career as a basketball player.

Teaching is a skill that many people underappreciated. Some think they are too busy or too important to teach someone something. Growing up, I was fortunate to have loving, caring parents who taught me many things. I also had role models who were older than me who I also learned a great deal from. The exposure that I received at a young age began to show as I got older. I would watch my peers and notice how competent I was in comparison as a result of all I was taught by my elders. And just as it was done for me, I often do things without the intent of receiving any benefit. Sometimes when people do things for free or for little compensation, it is possible to just want to do something for someone out of the kindness of your heart.

I used to ask my mother from time to time, "Why does it seem like I always extend myself to try and help people, but then when I am in need, it seems as if no one wants to help me?" She would smile at me and motivate me to continue to do what I was doing. She would encourage me by telling me my work was not going unnoticed. She would convince me that true rewards come from the glory of God. I almost reached a point in my life when I was like, "F*ck it, I am going to treat people just how they treat me."

I began to tell myself that I was going to lie, cheat, and steal from everybody, just as many people had done to me. I then started to monitor myself. This is when I realized that these thoughts I was expressing were out of pure frustration and anger. I once again turned to my Lord and Savior Jesus Christ and asked him to give me strength and a kind heart to continue to make provisions for those who were in need of uplifting and positive motivation. Even still at age twenty-four, I often reached points in my life when I lost sight of the importance of teaching, motivating, and helping others. When I reach those points in my life, it isn't long before God touches me once again and says, "JR, continue to do what you're doing. I see everything."

If someone were to ask me, "JR, why do you do the things you do? Why do you take the time out to give back and to speak to the youth about your life and things they should focus on in their lives as they continue to mature as young adults?" I would have a simple response. In the deep depths of my heart, I truly do believe that God sees all things, and that every time I reach out to a group of kids, there is always at least one youth who appreciates my efforts. If I speak to a group of a hundred kids at one time and only one of them truly appreciates my message and my lessons, then that is all I need in the whole world to feel happy and accomplished. So to all the aspiring role models out there, I want to encourage you, just like my mother encouraged me. Keep doing what you're doing. Your work is not and will never go unnoticed.

It is possible that you may get to a point when you feel as if no one's watching. Believe that God is watching your every footstep. If you truly believe in this, then the gratifying feeling you receive in knowing you're doing a deed for the greater good is all you need to find your own personal true happiness.

If you are searching for a reason to give back to the community you came from and other communities in general, think of your contribution toward society and being a role model. To some, this may not be important, but to those who understand the relevance of good role models, I encourage you to spread your leadership qualities in each and every community you come into contact with. Hall of Fame legend John Wooden said it best in his book, *A Lifetime of Observations and Reflections On and Off the Court*. "Being a role model is the most powerful form of education. Youngsters need good role models more than they need critics" (Wooden, 5). Too many times in our world, young people and people in general face so much scrutiny from their peers and spectators.

There is a difference between constructive criticism and belittling somebody. When we constructively critique someone's personality, we have the good intent of teaching them about themselves and helping them develop ways to strengthen their weakness. On the other hand, belittling someone can only bring down their self-confidence. This has no positive effect on that person's psyche, therefore it is socially counterproductive. As athletes, whether we like it or not, we are leaders and role models in the communities where we are recognized. This is evident in today's society, as kids are growing up wanting to look and act like the characters they see on television every day.

The installment of the NBA dress code to and from games is an example of the league's recognition of the social responsibility and professionalism that is admired by NBA fans. So many people, young and old, see these players traveling to games. For this reason, the NBA recognizes the importance of upholding a clean-cut image. After all, the NBA is a business like any other. It has to maintain a respectable reputation, just as every other professional league and corporate organization tries to.

I am a firm believer in the law of reciprocity. Individuals respond to a positive action with a corresponding positive action. When I was younger, I was fortunate to have many good role models in my life. These people taught me many things. I used to tell myself that when I got older, I would set an example for the next generation just like an example was set for me. Above all, "There is a law of nature that says there are three things we want most: happiness, freedom, and peace of mind. These concepts are always attained when we give them to others" (Wooden 1997, 15).

If you have ever done something for someone else and wondered why you even bothered helping them, use this quote John Wooden said to us as inspiration to institute these considerate gestures. So many people spend an entire lifetime seeking happiness, thinking that they will find it in superficial things. For women, a lot of times they think that happiness may come from attaining a wealthy man or someone who can provide for them. For men, this happiness is sought after in materialistic items and positional status. While these things certainly can make us feel temporarily competent, they are not and never will be a true indication of happiness.

Humans were socially constructed to live together and provide for each other. In the Bible, Eve came from the rib of Adam. She was literally derived from his flesh and blood, hence a dependency was birthed since the start of time. Nothing in our universe happens by itself. Everything has a dependency on something else. Sunrise could never exist without a period of dark night. Tsunamis would not occur without the earth's crust moving, which causes earthquakes. A sperm cannot fertilize without the involvement of a female egg. All of these examples prove that in order for things to successfully take place, a dependency is necessary. Our youth of tomorrow depends on the legacy that was started before them. As generations come and go, there are some things that transcend into the next generation and others that fade into obscurity. How do you want to be remembered? What legacy will you leave for your ancestors and their children thereafter?

A message to my aspiring future star athletes: If and when you reach elite athletic performance, understand that the lifestyle of an elite athlete is two-fold. First, you must train harder than most and strive to be the best. Second, you must provide an example for other aspiring athletes who will follow in your footsteps.

> Superstars who don't want the responsibility that comes with public acclaim don't have that choice. They are role models whether they like it or not; they cannot simply announce that they intend to shirk their responsibility. They are role models either good or bad. So are you. So am I." (Wooden 1997, 26)

Sports in today's world is internationally recognized. The athletes we see on TV and in advertisements are internationally recognized more than ever before. Some athletes choose to set bad examples. They do things they know are wrong. They will even break rules intentionally because of their arrogance and failure to recognize their social public acclaim.

On May 7, 2002, Allen Iverson, one of the NBA's most famous athletes, was asked in an interview about his failure to come to basketball practice. Although the media used this rant as a sports parody, the example it set for millions of youths who admire AI changed the minds of many who began questioning the importance of practice.

Allen Iverson is one of the greatest combo guards in the history of basketball. I would never take that away from him. No one should. His numbers speak for themselves. However, his attitude, the way he dressed and carried himself, and the way he dealt with the media was the cause for him being ostracized out of the National Basketball Association.

I personally believe one's attire, use of language, or views on political injustices should not be a reflection of the type of individual they are. Becoming a professional athlete is a decision and a privilege. With this privilege comes great responsibility. Before athletes are brought into any respected professional league, they are given conduct guidelines that specifically state how to act and interact with fans, media, and all other prospects. When we choose to be socially defiant, the effect of this is sometimes expulsion, and in the worst-case scenarios, excommunication.

What kind of leader do you wish to be? What legacy will you leave for future generations? How will you be remembered? These are all things to take into account with each and every action you take in your life. Remember, all of your actions have a reaction on someone else. Just when you think you're getting away with something, there is someone watching from the corner of their eye. It may be from the far distance of hindsight, but nevertheless, what you do in the dark will always come out in the light.

CHAPTER 8

Inmanology 101

The Five Correct Concepts for Success in Athletics
Formula for Success in College Athletics

1. Coaching
2. Chemistry
3. Captains
4. Carryover
5. Capable Athletes

In John Wooden's book *Pyramid of Success*, he developed a formula of keywords that he believes are ingredients toward one's individual achievement. Similar to that Idea, I have developed a formula for overall success in athletics. The Five Cs, as I like to call it, are the necessary intangibles collegiate athletic teams and professional teams need in order to be successful. Now I will break down each "C" and describe how it applies to success in basketball.

1. Coaching

Coaching is arguably the most valuable asset of any sports organization. The job of a coach is a unique position to fill, requiring leadership qualities, management skills, strategic proficiencies, and basketball knowledge. Coaches on the college level have so much responsibility, as their job extends far beyond just coaching kids during games. In college, many kids are away from their families and loved ones for the first time. A good college basketball coach creates ways to make the kid feel some sense of involvement. After all, when you play sports on an elite level, your teammates and your coaches become your extended family.

From a managerial position, you have to identify each player's role on the team so everyone knows what contributions they will be expected to perform. Bringing together an entire team of intricate parts can be a difficult task. This is why it is so important to have assistant coaches who can help with recruiting to bring in an array of natural talent. Accountability, dependability, reliability, and consistency are some of the themes that good coaches teach players. With these words manifested in a coach's locker room, the players will respect him, they will respect themselves, and most importantly, they will respect each other.

The last part of being a good coach is strategy or game plan. Every successful coach has a system that they are known for. Jim Boeheim's notorious 2-3 zone has become one of the most feared defenses to play against. Coach John Caliparie's "dribble drive offense" is starting to become mainstream. His framework allows fast-tempo transitional offense quick guards to penetrate gaps and take easy scoring opportunities. When coaches stick to their strategies, consistency is established. This provides a secure atmosphere, which in turn raises the team's prestige and confidence.

2. Chemistry

You see it all the time, the topic of interpersonal chemistry. There is a quote in the Rutgers University men's locker room that says, "You can do more with less when talent fails to work hard." This is indeed a fact. From a recruitment perspective, each and every kid who is brought into a program is made aware of the rules and regulations of that program. If a player decides to attend a school, he must comply with the rules that are put in place.

Good coaches facilitate opportunities for players to work on their relationships. Over the course of a long season, successful teams use practices and games to develop or enhance their chemistry. Without chemistry, teams with good talent will produce marginal results, and teams with average or below talent will perform below average.

3. **Captains**

This is what every team needs but doesn't have. Not just by position or rank, captains are natural-born leaders. Leadership is another important intangible in collegiate athletics. Captains provide direction and accountability for the program. When new players come into a program, the captain's job is to make the transition smooth and provide an example of how to act and interact within the program. Usually, your captains are seniors, but in situations where teams don't have seniors, anyone who has demonstrated leadership qualities on or off the court can serve as a captain or leader of a team.

With no captains, there is no leadership on the team. It's like having a car with no gas. Obviously, there are exceptions to this paradigm. There have been times when successful teams have limited leadership but still win games. Sometimes having an abundance of elite natural athletes is enough for a team to get by. The less leadership you have on a team, the more natural athleticism and ability you must have to compensate for the lack of leadership.

4. **Carryover**

Carryover can be defined as the consistency a team has to perform at a high level of play over a given period of time. Sometimes teams start off great early in the season but then hit a wall halfway through. You may see some players who are superstars in practice but only role players in the game. Developing consistency in sports promotes success because it ensures the idea of readiness and efficiency.

Coaching and leadership also help carryover. Players need to be motivated after each day they perform to continue to execute. Each day if we focus on execution, our carryover will transcend into the next practice or the next game.

5. <u>Capability</u>

This variable goes hand in hand with chemistry. Each position has specific qualities that make players in that position effective. In the business world, each job has specific skills employees are required to have. There are a few commonalities most successful basketball teams have that I would like to focus on:

A. Floor Generals - players who can direct on offense and create scoring opportunities.
B. Shooters - players who can hit shots for various points on the floor.
C. Slashers - players who can attack the basket and finish plays in transition.
D. Rebounders - players who can control the offensive and defensive glass.
E. Defenders - players who can either block or steal the ball from offensive players.

Think of the construction of a professional athletic club like a car. Each player has an attribute that helps the team engine run. Ask yourself, what would a supreme engine be without supreme oil and supreme gas? You would have to remember not to try and pull off without the wheels, because a car with no wheels is like a king with no rings. The brakes, windshield wipers, and all other vehicular parts provide further support and assistance. To give you a more in-depth perspective on this last aspect of the Five Cs, let's take a great team in sports history and analyze its roster and role distribution.

2011 Dallas Mavericks NBA Finals Champions

Player and Role on Team

Floor Generals
1. <u>Jason Kidd</u>: Veteran Hall of Fame potential candidate who demonstrates elite leadership experience on and off the court. He is a visionary. He controlled the tempo of the Mavericks' offense with his mind.
2. <u>Dirk Nowitzki</u>: The most efficient offensive seven-footer in the history of the game, Dirk was the catalyst for the Mavericks' attack all the way through the NBA Finals last season.
3. <u>JJ Barea</u>: Role player with exceptional skills. He learned under the leadership of Jason Kidd and provided acrobatic energy that helped fuel the Mavericks' transition offense.

Shooters
1. <u>Dirk Nowitzki:</u> He is the purest shooting big man in the history of the NBA.
2. <u>Jason Terry:</u> This combo guard is capable of getting big buckets at crucial parts of the game.
3. <u>Peja Stojakovic:</u> He is one of the top five most efficient European three-point shooters in the history of the NBA.

Slashers
1. <u>Deshawn Stevenson:</u> Also a capable shooter, but he is at his best when he is a force driving straight to the basket in transition.
2. <u>Corey Brewer:</u> He jumps with the best of them.
3. <u>Caron Butler:</u> He was injured for the entire NBA finals, but when healthy, he was one of the top ten slashers in the NBA during the 2010–2011 season.

Rebounders
1. <u>Tyson Chandler</u>: He is one of the best rebounders over seven feet in the NBA.
2. <u>Brendan Haywood</u>: He added support to provide strength on the offensive and defensive glass.
3. <u>Jason Kidd:</u> He is also the best rebounding pure point guard in the history of the game.

Defenders
1. <u>Shawn Marion</u>: At six foot nine, he is a versatile combo forward who could guard any and every position on the basketball court if necessary.
2. <u>Tyson Chandler:</u> He was one of the best defensive rebounders in the Western Conference in the 2010–2011 NBA season. Chandler gave this team rebounding and shot-blocking ability combined with length intangibles that can't be measured by statistical data.
3. <u>Brendan Haywood</u>: More often than not, he was the largest man on the court during the 2010–2011 NBA Finals. Haywood was a force to be reckoned with. If at any point in time the opposition managed to penetrate the swarming hands of the Dallas Mavericks' defense, Haywood was there to block shots, take charges, and body up opposing offensive players.

Personally, as a basketball fan and fellow professional, I believe this is one of the top five best basketball teams in NBA history. You must give extreme kudos to Mark Cuban and the entire Dallas Maverick front office for putting together such an elite group of superior basketball players. Reverting back to my earlier analogy of professional athletic teams and cars, the Dallas Mavericks certainly had all the finest parts that together enabled a running motor that touched the hearts of Maverick fans, basketball fans, and many others across the world.

There are many other teams that we could talk about that also have a balanced player/role status that led them to success. Successful organizations have commonalities with other successful organizations, like the arrangement of role deposition and the effective use of it. These teams accomplish team goals. In sports, the goal that joins prestigious teams together is winning. Everyone wants to win. Since the beginning of mankind, the desire for man to be victorious in all of his endeavors has been embedded in our spirits. If our primary goal in life is to win, then we should strive to surround ourselves with other people that have the same aspirations!

CHAPTER 9

The Perks of Being a Ballplayer

Basketball is not only a sport, it's a lifestyle. There are standards we must live up to, but if managed correctly, the accommodations can be most accommodating: first-class airplane tickets, five-star hotel suites around the world, and social acclaim. These are all examples of positive attributes acquired through professional basketball. This game has opened doors in my life that will never close. I have networked with people who will change my life forever.

There was nothing greater than a trip I took to Israel in the summer of 2010. I called that trip my "Israel Excursion." This was a turning point in my life. It was through these happenings that I was able to find myself and my purpose in life. I firmly believe God makes people for certain reasons. God designed the structure of my bones and muscles to move in such a manner that I am able to play the game of basketball with elite proficiency. It was no accident that he made me six feet nine inches tall, long, and lean. When I was younger, I used to question if my purpose in life was to become a professional basketball player. It wasn't until I prayed on it and saw Jesus in Israel that I started believing in my fate wholeheartedly. I will try to provide a quick abstract of my Israel Excursion so you can see a glimpse of my life-changing experience.

I woke up one morning and received a telephone call from one of my most trusted advisors. He said, "I'm going to get you in the NBA."

When the Air Comes Out of the Ball

I still had groggy cols in the corners of my eyes. It was six o'clock in the morning, and I was yet to even brush my teeth or look in the mirror. My doorbell rang. I answered the door in flip-flops and a bathrobe, and his first words to me were, "Are you ready to go to the NBA?" It was like a dream. I looked into his eyes and saw something. I saw a man who believed in me. He believed that if I was connected to the right people, I could achieve something that many say is impossible. That meant something to me. I told "Mr. Jacket" that I appreciated his enthusiasm so much that I would follow in his footsteps. I went with him to meet one of the chaplains of the Boston Celtics, Reverend Bill Alexon. He was a God-fearing, special person. He called me one day and told me how he had put together a professional basketball religious charity organization called "Sports Power International." This team featured some of the most Christian professional athletes I have ever come into contact with. Together, our mission was to travel to Israel and reach out to the Israeli community.

We used our professional basketball charisma to spread the word of God and demonstrate America's support for the Israeli people. I watched Alan Houston read from the Holy Bible on a pillar outside the Church of Mensa Christi.

Figure 16: JR inside the Church of Mensa Christi

I broke bread with Dwight Howard Sr. in the King David Hotel in Jerusalem. The Lord God opened my eyes to the depths of the Dead Sea and enabled my stomach to eat fresh salmon captured and delivered straight from the Mediterranean. On our Sunday Sabbath day, we communed outside of the Dome of the Rock. It was beautiful to see people from all religious backgrounds coming together and praying. There were hundreds if not thousands of people from various backgrounds, cultures, and faiths. I saw a Hasidic Jewish man fellowshipping directly next to a Christian man who was absorbed by the Holy Spirit. At that point in time for me and for all who were assembled, our religious differences didn't matter. We were all in a place that was unified by one Lord, one Faith, and one Baptism. Yes, we may have referenced him by using different names: God, Jehovah, Yahweh, Messiah, etc. Regardless of the name used to describe "God," we were all functioning under the belief that we must give reference to a higher being that is greater than man.

The Israel Excursion was an experience that changed my life. I was able to get in touch with my intrapersonal spirit. I felt Jesus's holistic spirit. I was blessed to meet other God-fearing Christians who had an impact on my professional basketball experience. I am eternally thankful to all who made my Israel Excursion possible. It was a voyage that shall never be forgotten. Wow, what a perk of being a ballplayer.

In 2011, I took a flight out to Las Vegas to compete in a tryout for the Korean Basketball League (KBL). I stayed at the MGM Grand Casino and watched people gamble their lives away. I was amazed at how many people operated under the assumption that they could get rich by rolling dice or holding a lucky hand in poker. Some people spend their life savings on a weekend in Vegas. It's crazy if you ask me. I was never that shallow. I like to spend my money, but I don't want to waste it.

Thank God I was never a gambler, or I would have lost all of my money. Las Vegas is a very fast place. Well, it's fast but slow at the same time. There are no clocks on the streets, and the lack of humidity in the air makes the day drag a little bit. The night is filled with fluster and mischief. Some find this lifestyle appealing. Personally, I find it distasteful. It's cool to experience the club scenes, pop bottles, and go back to your hotel room with different girls on different days at different times. At times, you may find yourself in circumstances that are highly convincing. Whenever I find myself in situations that compromise my upbringing, I just think, "What would Jesus do? What would my parents do?" This thought process does not always cause me to make the right decisions, but it allows me to sense whether the decision I'm making is right or wrong. With that being said, I always enjoy myself when I go to Las Vegas. After all, "What happens in Vegas, stays in Vegas!"

There's not a greater feeling in the world than championships. You love it. You dream about it. You prepare for it. You work hard for an entire season for it. Then when you win, your body feels gratification like the birth of a newborn baby. Winning in sports brings so many character traits out of you. It gives you a burning desire to achieve something. Self-esteem is elevated through personal achievement. It's more than the plaques hanging on the wall, the seven-foot trophies decorating your bedroom, or the diamond championship pinky rings. When you win, you know that your efforts contributed to something that was recognized as being superior to your peers and opponents. Competition in itself is a perk that most athletes fail to recognize. In life, there are always competitors. There is someone playing defense, trying to stop you from scoring your goal. Your life can be broken down into quarters, halves, or any time reference you choose. During this time period, it is up to you to perform. This is the nature of the human being. Since the beginning of time, there has always been opposition. When opposing forces meet, there is always someone or something that will win, and someone or something that will lose.

In outer space when two opposing asteroids cross coordinates, one is smashed into several smaller pieces. On Earth, when boxers fight in a match, one guy is going to leave the ring the winner, and the other will leave the ring having lost. Nothing is ever equal. This is why you have to work hard in life to receive a desirable position in society. Our society is constructed like a sport. There are different leagues throughout the world, and all these leagues have different rules. Within these leagues, there is one winner, and after the season is over, all other competitors are losers who strive in the next season to be like the winners from the last season.

There is a competitive force in all of our institutions and organizations. Many times when people retire from sports, they find jobs where their skills and principles are needed. Athletes have a proven work ethic, which many businesses need. This is why I encourage collegiate athletes to stay in school. With a degree, athletic experience, and a work ethic, you can go a long way in this world. These are gifts that have been given to us. The glory of God enabled you to run that fast and jump that high; now use these skills to your benefit and show God's works unto the world. When you compete, use this as your motivation for elite achievement. Represent yourself and your family with pride. Always be proud of who you are and never forget where you came from. Walk upright at all times and never show any signs of weakness or inferiority. We do this as athletes because this is what we prepare for. This is yet another perk of being a ballplayer.

There are many other perks I could sample to demonstrate the abundant lifestyles of professional athletes. The point is that the exposure you receive from playing ball provides you with everything you need to direct your path and have an upright, noble lifespan. Leave your mark on society. Provide a framework for others that will change lives. The life of a professional athlete is admirable. So many depend on you for your services. And in gracious cases, you have the support of a fan base that embraces you with love and appreciation.

So what about respect? Respect is a word that is used incorrectly. Many who use the word think they know its meaning, yet their actions beg to differ. If you have no respect for the game, how could you expect to get respect from the game? Respect your teammates, respect your coaches, respect your body, and respect yourselves. It is your duty to remain physically fit throughout your professional experience. You should eat healthy, stretch continuously, and push your muscles past exhaustion. Not only is physical fitness vital for athletic prominence, it also has several positive long-term health effects.

Developing a physical fitness workout schedule institutes a work ethic. When we work our bodies, we strengthen our immune systems, which in turn can help fight off diseases. There are many workout plans you could do on a daily basis to enhance your overall physical fitness. One thing I like to maintain is my cardiovascular system. This is one of the most essential factors that an athlete needs to be most effective. The method for establishing a respectable cardiovascular heart rate is easy. Commit yourself to a period of time: one month, two months, three months. Imagine yourself and your progress after the first of each month. Develop a plan to bring about that change, and don't stop working until you see what you thought you saw in that picture.

If at this point in time you are still struggling to develop this plan, let me provide you with an example.

Example:

Jason is a sixteen-year-old high school running back from Kensington, New Jersey. This all-county running back ran a 4.6-second forty-yard dash at the 2011 Collegiate Running Back Elite Football Combine. His goal was to run a 4.4. Jason's daily diet consists of fast food and candies; the beverages he drank all have high fructose corn syrup, alcohol, and many other unnatural flavors; and his pre-workout routine lacks discipline and organization. How can Jason cut his forty-yard dash time by two-tenths of a second or more by training camp next season?

Resolution:

First, Jason estimated the date for next year's Elite Running Back Combine to be in August 2012. For his seventeenth birthday, he asked his parents if he could spend the month of July at Uncle Chuckey's cabin in Long Eddy,

New York. For an entire month, Jason ran up sand mountains, chopped down trees, and sprinted through narrow, low-grass valleys.

He committed himself to a strict diet of fruits and berries with fresh spring water and thin-sliced cold cuts. He stretched for twenty-five minutes before and after every workout. He timed each drill and tried to beat that time the next time around.

That very next spring, Jason set a combine record when he ran the forty-yard dash in 4.19 seconds. After his performance, a reporter asked, "Jason, how did you manage to cut almost three-tenths of a second off of your forty-yard dash time and set a combine record in one off-season?"

Jason's answer was, "I imagined myself being the fastest running back in the country. I painted the picture in my head and then worked hard at making the image in the picture become the image you see here today."

The example of Jason Bedford symbolizes the commitment and responsibility that comes with being an elite athlete. Jason had to respect his mind and body in order to reach his goals. During his escape to Long Eddy, he found something: the passion and dedication required to be an elite athlete.

He motivated himself to get up early every morning and go to sleep early every night because it meant that much to him. He finally understood what it took to be great. He learned what he had to do in order to take his game to the next level. This is a beautiful story of work ethic. If you don't work hard in sports, then you have no respect for the game. That's what this chapter is all about: respect and the lack thereof.

To my fellow professional athletes, go on about your business. Represent like you know how. Be proud of what you have worked for and the skills that God has blessed you with. Do not function with haste, gluttony, pride, or glory. Promote prominence over arrogance and esteem over jealousy and envy. What good is a ballplayer without perks? What good are the perks without the ballplayer?"

CHAPTER 10

From Black Kicks to Hard Bottoms

I have spent a large portion of this book on the probabilities of athletes making it professionally versus the odds of them falling short of their dreams. Now I would like to take you through some examples of athletes who had stellar professional careers but then faced hardship after retirement. Today our society only focuses on glitz and glamour. We are so quick to hear in the papers when an athlete signs a big-time contract or when he or she purchases a large, expensive item. There is a transition period from when an athlete is playing at a high competitive level to when their playing days are over. During this time, some athletes take everything they have acquired over a long career and put it to good use. Others breeze through an entire career but never obtain any assets or knowledge that promotes their success beyond sports.

It has been estimated that approximately 78 percent of all NFL players and 60 percent of all NBA players face bankruptcy or economic hardship within five years post-retirement. These numbers are both embarrassing and shameful. Although each athlete has different reasons for this plummet, their financial destruction all have similar reasons as to why they eventually become broke. Overall, not having a game plan for how you will manage your money and what you will do with your life is the reason for these abysmal numbers.

To get a better understanding of how multimillionaires can lose all of their revenue, let's look at a few examples of former athletes who have bit the financial bullet after their playing days come to a halt.

1. Evander Holyfield:
Four-time Heavyweight Champion of the World
Dubbed as the "Real Deal"
Estimated lifetime earnings: $250 million

- He had a deal with Diet Coke.
- Launched several businesses such as:
    - Real Deal Grill, an electric cooking appliance
    - Real Deal Boxing, a video game
    - Real Deal Records, a record label
- Had TV, radio, and other media appearances

A father of eleven children, Holyfield, when asked about his financial struggles, admits that he is not "broke," just not "liquid." It has been reported that the heavyweight champ was around $9,000 behind in court-ordered child support payments. As a result, the banks foreclosed his $10-million home. Even a landscaping firm says the former champ owes them $500,000 for yard work. It seems as if Evander's life is far different from the days when he was dancing around in the ring.

2. Johnny Unitas:
Hall of Fame quarterback, three-time MVP,
Super Bowl champion, and *ten-time Pro Bowl selection.*
Estimated lifetime earnings: $4 million

Many say Mr. Unitas is one of the best quarterbacks of all time. Out of many of the records he broke, possibly the most astounding record he holds is a streak of 47 games played in a row throwing a touchdown pass.

- He made some money as a TV commentator for CBS.
- He also invested in a chain of bowling establishments.
- He is an owner of a Prime Rib restaurant.
- He is an owner of an air freight company.
- He has Florida real estate investments.

This alias hero and all-time great football player filed for bankruptcy in 1991. He died eleven years later with a lawsuit from his estate hanging over all of his businesses.

3. Sheryl Swoopes:
Three-time gold medal Olympian, three-time MVP for the WNBA, and first pro women's basketball player.
Estimated lifetime earnings: $50 Million

Swoopes, the Michael Jordan of the WNBA, put out her own Nike deal for the Jordan-inspired "Air Swoopes" brand. Swoopes, a marketing machine, at one point was the face of the WNBA, but her fortunes didn't last. She filed for bankruptcy in 2004, resulting from mismanagement by her agents and lawyers. She owed approximately $750,000.

4. Lawrence Taylor:
New York Giants MVP, sack leader, Hall of Famer, and two-time Super Bowl champ.
Estimated lifetime earnings: $50 million

After LT retired, his fancy lifestyle continued. He was and will forever be remembered for being a man who likes to live lavishly. Lawrence had an obsession with women as well as an addiction to cocaine and alcoholism. He was arrested three times for drug possession. The IRS investigated him for filing a false tax return.

Inevitably, he finally declared bankruptcy in 1998. One year later, the Pro Football Hall of Fame inducted him as a reward for cleaning up his act.

5. Jack Clark:
MLB player since 1975
Estimated lifetime earnings: $20 million

$11.4 million and assets of $4.8 million.
Owned eighteen cars.

Of Mr. Clark's eighteen automobiles, he suffered from a failure to complete the car payments on seventeen of them. When you talk about a man with expensive habits, you talk about the all-time baseball great Jack Clark.

These are some of the most well-known athletes in America in the past century. Kudos to every one of them for their contributions to American history on the playing field. It is somewhat shameful that these individuals failed to maintain a universally respectable social status after retirement.

The truth is that most of us would make the same mistakes that celebrities make. This is why it is important to focus on the principle of life after sports. First, establish a plan, then use tools that will help your dream become a reality. This will lead to economic prosperity and financial competence.

There are two major issues I can point out that I have seen as direct causes of bankruptcy. The first issue is what I like to call the "biting off more than you can chew epidemic." This occurs when people try to live up to others' standards and purchase more liabilities and possessions than they can afford. The example of Jack Clark's purchase of eighteen cars is a perfect example of biting off more than you can chew. You can only drive one car at a time. Furthermore, the maintenance of a $700,000 car is going to bring up its total cost by well over a million dollars just for one vehicle. At the time Clark purchased his vehicles, he probably never anticipated a day would come when his income would stop but his bills wouldn't.

The second problem I see a lot of athletes face is that they invest in private business ventures that they have little to no managerial knowledge of. This is a mistake that many people who try to establish small businesses make. I took a business management course in college, and I'll never forget something my instructor taught me. "Ninety percent of all small businesses fail. When starting your own business, never attempt to start a business you cannot do yourself." Well, maybe someone should have told Scottie Pippin this before he attempted to manage a private jet airline. Too often, you see people invest in products and businesses that they have no knowledge about. This is an extremely risky way to do business, and more often than not, if you choose this method for building revenue, your results will not be desirable.

On the flip side, there are also notable athletes who have managed to maintain their wealth and use it to invest in promising business ventures. These are the people we as young entrepreneurs and athletes should strive to emulate. These people should not only be appreciated for their efforts on the playing field, but also for the decisions they made when the air came out of the ball.

1. Magic Johnson:

- Ownership interests in Starbucks (105 locations).
- Part ownership of many *TGI Friday's* locations and Loews Movie Theaters.
- Part owner of the Los Angeles Lakers, as well as a handful of other business interests.
- He owns a travel franchise, *Magic Johnson Travel Group* which focuses on attracting multicultural franchisees that cater to the minority travel segment.
- He owns The Magic Johnson Foundation which supports people with HIV/AIDS and provides scholarships for inner-city kids.

I respect and glorify Magic Johnson for not only being a superb businessman, but also for rising above his circumstances. After being diagnosed with HIV, he used his formidable reputation to create ways to help those who also have been inflicted with the virus and may not have the means or confidence to proactively do something about it.

2. Keyshawn Johnson:

- Super Bowl Champion
- Best-selling author and ESPN analyst is also the CEO of First Picks Management, a business development company with an emphasis on franchises.
- Keyshawn's company opened several *Panera Bread* franchises throughout California.

Some remember Keyshawn for being a stunning athlete who preached the motto, "Just give me the damn ball." I will remember him for using his prolific demeanor as an asset that promoted business ventures beyond the game of football.

3. Jamal Mashburn:

- He owns 71 restaurants.
- Part owner of the Kentucky Derby horse, Buffalo Man.
- Part owner of Outback Steak House.

Made over $75 million during his basketball career, Mash decided not to rest on his laurels after his NBA career was over.

Mr. Mashburn could have rested on his laurels or his reputation from his most memorable season with the Dallas Mavericks in 1994. But instead, he used his career to catapult his life, giving him a future of longevity and financial freedom.

So now you have seen a few examples of athletes who were successful after their playing days were finished, as well as a few examples of some who have failed. Business and finance is only one aspect of life. Success is not solely evaluated by income or financial capital. The examples used earlier in this chapter provide just a glimpse of the harsh realities that most athletes have to face someday.

I for one never wanted to be a failed statistic. Money management is something I take very seriously. I am thankful that I have a fundamental understanding of finance, enough to determine what is a good investment and a bad investment. Always remember that it's not how much money you can make, it's all about how much money you can keep. I am confident that when my playing days are over, I will have a positive life ahead of me. I have invested years of knowledge and finance over the years to ensure that all of my future aspirations can be obtained someday. I work hard now for an ultimate payoff later.

Looking the Part

One of my most trusted mentors and avid supporters, Lincoln Sessoms, once told me, "JR, if you want to be a player, you've got to look like a player." He was trying to teach me that appearance is an indication of one's personal competence. I believe this same lesson can be applied in the world of work. Looking the part requires individuals who seek an occupation to carry themselves in a first-class, business professional way. There aren't any set rules on how to dress or conduct yourself, but there are unwritten rules that can increase your chances when hitting the job market.

The biggest and most obvious part of appearance is your face. When you walk into any establishment, it's the first thing people notice. It is important to get a sharp haircut and maintain a desirable hairstyle. This may seem unimportant, but believe it or not, a fresh haircut can take you a long way. When you keep your hair looking great, it lets people know that you're worth something and that you want to be somebody. It tells people that you respect yourself enough to wake up every morning, look in the mirror, and feel proud about how you represent yourself.

You want to get a good night's rest before interviewing or going to work, because late nights will show under your eyes the next day. No one wants to go to work looking and feeling groggy. That's why it is important to get a lot of rest, then wake up early in the morning so you can wash yourself thoroughly and begin your day.

Your attire is probably the second most important attribute in looking the part. We live in an extremely judgmental society. This is a sad but true statement. Before you even open your lips, people are already making assumptions about the type of person you are based on your physical appearance. This is why you need to take pride in what you wear every day.

When you go to work (according to the dress code, of course), remember to iron your shirts with starch to keep the creases sharp. If you wear suits, take them to the cleaners to get them professionally cared for. Invest in an appealing pair of shoes that complement your work clothing. Be sure to purchase ties that also complement your personality and the outfits you will be wearing them with. If you are a white-collar worker, make sure you get a leather briefcase that glistens when you walk in the sun.

It may seem like I'm being practical, but trust me, these things are noticed and they can get you farther in life than you think. Take pride when you step out of the house each day. If you are married or living with loved ones, don't be afraid to ask, "How do I look?" Your family will be the most honest with you on whether or not you are looking your best. To all the youth who are still reading this portion of the book and haven't browsed through it, I encourage you to get fresh and always dress your best.

Utilizing Your Name and Networks

This portion of the chapter will focus on all athletes and those who aspire to become athletes, including the advantage you have over the average Joe. Once you have climbed the ranks of professional sports, consider yourself an elite public figure. People know who you are. People who you may not know or have ever seen before know what you do, who you hang out with, and where. While this could seem a bit creepy at first, I believe an athlete should use this social acclaim to his or her advantage. Take this opportunity as a way to develop a reputation of prosperity. Make people believe in you and not just in what you can do on the playing field.

When you travel, realize who and what you represent. You represent your family, the team you are playing for, and most importantly, yourself. Take this as an opportunity to meet new people who share your interests. You never know what that person can do for you in the future. There is a networking theory called "the strength of weak ties" that examines the importance of networking.

> The individuals with more weak ties have greater opportunities for mobility. Lots of weak ties provide a "seedbed of individual autonomy." People with many weak ties live up to the expectations of several others in different places and at different times, which makes it possible to preserve an inner core—to withhold inner attitudes while conforming to various expectations. People with strong ties share norms so thoroughly that little effort is needed to gauge the intentions of others." (Granovetter, Analytic Tech)

When I first heard of this theory, I was studying communication during my sophomore year in college. It was hard for me to grasp this subject matter because I was functioning under the wrong assumption. I thought that it was through your stronger networks that you would be able to be connected or linked to a job position for which you fit the requirements. I was shocked when I found out that the truth was actually the opposite of my assumption. Athletes come into contact with so many people on an everyday basis. This is why it is extremely important to always look the part and establish long-lasting networks. You just never know who you might meet that could change your life. It is always better to enter every interaction thinking that this person is going to be a positive influence on your life. When you treat people with respect and put your best foot forward, they inevitably will perceive you as someone capable of merging from the sports world into the business world.

Finding Your Passion Outside of Sports

One of the most disheartening deficiencies I have seen in my professional sports career is athletes who have "sports tunnel vision." They have no other passion, hobby, or skill that they enjoy doing outside of sports. Sports are fun, don't get me wrong, but sports isn't life. There is indeed life after sports.

The average professional basketball career lasts four years. That number is probably smaller for even more aggressive contact sports like football or boxing. Let's say you defeat the odds and have a ten-year professional sports career. You entered into the pros at twenty-three, and now you are thirty-three years old and retired. If the average life expectancy is well over sixty-five these days, what do you suggest an athlete who has sports tunnel vision do for the remaining fifty-plus years of his or her life? Most of the time, this answer is not appealing. Many get caught up in drugs and street life and don't get the opportunity to see themselves grow old.

This is why I want to encourage the youth of today to develop another passion outside of sports. Do something that you enjoy doing or something that can impact or affect the community. If you ever do make it big, invest in projects and business ventures that you can relate to in some way. There are two notable pro ballplayers I want to talk about to exemplify this point I'm trying to make.

1. **Trevor Ariza:** NBA World Champion Trevor Ariza opened up a series of Buffalo Wild Wings restaurants. Ariza is using

his business venture ideas to raise money and awareness of asthma-related illnesses. Trevor was born with asthma and has a sentimental attachment to this health issue, which affects hundreds of thousands across the globe. I too was born with asthma, so I can relate to him on this one.

2. **Dikembe Mutombo:** This NBA Hall of Fame humanitarian realizes the healthcare epidemic that faces his native continent of Africa. Among many efforts he has made to help this problem, his hospital in Congo is probably the most notable. One of the NBA's all-time leading shot blockers, Mutombo understands that there are many who need his help. He used the revenue he earned over a long career to help bring about change to a community that needs it badly.

These are just two examples of pro athletes who have taken advantage of their God-given talent and used it to improve and uplift their communities. The point is this, ladies and gentlemen: what good is being great at something if you take nothing away from it? The true indication of a well-rounded, skilled professional is someone who does something with great expertise and then provides an example for others as to how things are done and should be done for those who come after. Sports is more than being able to kick a fifty-yard field goal or hit forty home runs in a season. Being a skilled player is just one aspect of athletics. Off the field, it is just as imperative to provide an example for how things are done and to educate those who aspire to be like you. Once you have achieved success in sports, the task of becoming a recognizable public icon is all up to you!

CHAPTER 11

JR's Final Thoughts

If you can imagine it, then you can see it. If you can see it, then it can be obtained. I'm talking about vision and personal achievement. Believe in all of your talents and abilities. Wholeheartedly commit yourself toward the further advancement of your disposition in society. There is no doubt that you will face adversity. It is in the nature of man to face hardship and jeopardy, but it is also in the nature of man to persevere and overcome obstacles.

Be confident in all of your endeavors. If the going gets tough and you begin to question the possibilities of achievement, invest yourself with confidence and optimism. I firmly believe that anything that is possible, is probable, when you're living a life of optimism. Why not see the glass of life as half full rather than half empty? Besides, what we have is what we have. If we work hard, then what we desire is what we will receive.

Surround yourself with people, places, and things that will raise your self-esteem. Friends, family, and trusted acquaintances are important providers of esteem. They encourage your efforts and believe in your capabilities. Gravitate toward those characters who give you positive energy. Also, you should reciprocate positive esteem when you come across people during your daily interactions.

I'm not saying that you should want to be liked by everyone, but you certainly want to surround yourself with individuals who respect your savvy. This is simple practical knowledge, a suggestion for how one could direct his existence. One can perceive this knowledge as guidelines for those who wonder how to manage their lives with ordinance, discipline, and ethical doctrine.

Don't believe the hype. Stay away from spreading rumors. Believe half of what you see and none of what you hear, because even visions can sometimes appear to be most obscure. Integrity is something that you must pray for. God gives it to us as a gift from heaven, but it is up to us to manifest it into our orderly conduct.

Congratulate your peers for their achievements. Converse with your partners and vocalize your gratification. When we tell people how we feel, that energy can reflect upon us. Remember that according to physics, energy is never lost, it is only transferred. If you want people to respect you, then you have to respect people. Good parents instill respect in their children. When two people respect each other, it is called mutual respect. The respect level factors into the conversation during each face-to-face encounter.

I want to give honor to God, who is at the head of my life. I want to thank my parents for making me the man I am today. I have been blessed with a huge support system that I cannot thank enough. I'd also like to thank my sister Jasmine who has listened to me during the busyness of life. To my grandmother, Annie Jewel Williams, I love you! It is your strength passed down the bloodline that enables me to get through tough times. To all of my coaches, each and every one of you taught me lessons that I will never forget. To my church family at Pilgrim Baptist Church in Nyack, New York: you are the strongest support system I have. My friends are real friends who stuck by me regardless of what others said about me. They defended me at times when ignorance attempted to defame my character. They believed in me. They always believed that I was special, and this gave me much strength. For that, I am forever thankful.

The good Lord has blessed me with a genuine church family. I embrace my brothers and sisters with peace, love, and happiness. I have traveled around the world and back again, and yet God has kept me safe and away from danger and harm. He has opened my eyes to doors that I could never have seen otherwise, exposing me to international and extraordinary experiences.

And now comes my next mission in life. At the time I am writing this paragraph, I stand six feet, nine inches tall, weigh two hundred and thirty-two pounds, and am just twenty-five years of age. My transition from high school to college allowed me to mature and gain superior knowledge. Then when I graduated college, I began to see a transition within myself into the man I have become today. This sequence has brought me to the point I am at right now. I will continue to play basketball until my bones cannot bear the brutality of the game any longer. All the while, I will commit myself to spread my message across the globe.

My message is this: Athletics is one of the main cornerstones in human society. If you are fortunate to have been blessed with some type of coordination or skill, use it to your advantage. Enhance your weaknesses and make them your strengths. Never lose sight of reality. Every dog will have its day. As much as I love the game of basketball, I know that there will come a day when I can play no further. I have used basketball as a window of opportunity. Who would have ever known that a rubber brown ball could bring me to my wildest dreams? Although I am proud of all of my success in athletics, I am equally gratified by my educational achievements. If you can run long distances and jump over hurdles and obstacles, then your mind can do just the same. For my athletes, if you take nothing else from this entire message, just ask yourselves this one question: What will I do when the air comes out of the ball?

REFERENCES

Boone, Thabiti. 2000. *Rising to the Occasion. A Student Athlete's Success on and off the Playing Field.* Thabiti Enterprises.

Byrne, Rhonda. 2006. *The Secret.* Beyond Words Publishing. Retrieved October 11, 2008, from http://en.wikipedia.org/ wiki/ The Law of Attraction.

Drea. "25 Rich Athletes Who Went Broke." Business Pundit. May 18, 2009. http://www.businesspundit.com/25-rich-athletes-who-went-broke/.

Granovetter, Mark. "The Strength of Weak Ties." Analytic Tech. Accessed November 4, 2011. http://www.analytictech.com/networks/weakties.htm.

Knowles, E. "Murphy's Law." The Oxford Dictionary of Phrase and Fable. *Oxford University Press*, (1962). Accessed September 25, 2009. http://www.encyclopedia.com.

Maher, Patrick. "Kuhn on Anomalies." The Structure of Scientific Revolutions Retrieved. *University of Chicago Press*, (1962). Accessed September 25, 2009. http:// patrick. maher1.net/270/lectures/kuhn.pdf.

Pinkett, Randal. 2007. *Campus CEO: The Student Entrepreneur's Guide to Launching a Multi-million Dollar Business.* Kaplan Publishing.

Gallagher, Sandy. "The Law of Vibration - Proctor Gallagher Institute." Proctor Gallagher Institute, January 3, 2017. https://www.proctorgallagherinstitute.com/6956/the-law-of-vibration.

Wooden, John, and Jay Carty. 2009. *Coach Wooden's Pyramid of Success: Building Blocks for a Better Life*. Regal.

Wooden, John, and Steve Jamison. 1997. *Wooden: A Lifetime of Observations and Reflections On and Off the Court*. McGraw Hill.

www.ingramcontent.com/pod-product-compliance
Lightning Source LLC
LaVergne TN
LVHW091545070526
838199LV00002B/211